Guitar one
PRESENTS

OPEN EARS

A JOURNEY THROUGH LIFE
WITH GUITAR IN HAND

BY
STEVE
MORSE

ESSAYS AND INSIGHTS ON
BEING A MUSICIAN

ISBN 1-57560-364-0

Copyright © 2001 Cherry Lane Music Company
International Copyright Secured   All Rights Reserved

Visit our website at www.cherrylane.com

INTRODUCTION

From 1982 through 1999, *Guitar for the Practicing Musician* set the pace for guitar and guitar playing for thousands of readers around the world. The magazine was an engaging, hands-on guide for guitarists eager to learn about their instruments and the players they admired. "We wanted to harness the power of the electric guitar," said founding editor John Stix, "and pump it through each page using words, pictures, and music."

During the 1980s, the magazine explored the views and techniques of such luminaries as Eddie Van Halen, Jeff Beck, Stevie Ray Vaughan, Steve Vai, Joe Satriani, George Lynch, and Nuno Bettencourt. This was a time of rapid changes for rock guitar, and *Guitar for the Practicing Musician* was there to help exploit new trends such as two-handed tapping, sweep picking, and whammy-bar technique.

Each month, *Guitar for the Practicing Musician* provided note-perfect transcriptions of the hottest contemporary and classic guitar-based songs. Never before had a guitar magazine included complete, authentically transcribed music. "Without music you're only getting half the picture!" the magazine's original ads proclaimed, a torn photo of Eddie Van Halen illustrating the point. Meanwhile, the magazine's pioneering use of tablature, a unique notational system designed specifically for guitarists, made that music accessible to guitarists of all levels.

In the '90s, *Guitar for the Practicing Musician* continued to track the cutting edge of guitar music and technology. The magazine's distinguished staff of high-profile columnists regularly presented new approaches to the guitar and tales of their experiences as professionals. As the alternative and grunge scenes rose to popularity, *Guitar* (the name was abridged mid-decade) was there again to keep readers informed of such unconventional players as Kurt Cobain, Jerry Cantrell, Billy Corgan, and Dimebag Darrell. An extensive new department called Gear Factory was also added, enabling readers to gain valuable insight into the nuts and bolts of their guitars, amps, effects, and other applicable tools of the trade. By the end of the decade, the "new metal" sounds of bands like Korn, Deftones, Sevendust, and Limp Bizkit were making their way into the pages of Guitar, bringing with them a focus on such hot topics as downtuning and 7-string axes.

Today, the magazine's sister publication, *GuitarOne*, carries on the tradition of covering the world's greatest guitarists and their music, as well as providing essential lessons, tips, and insights. On behalf of everyone who has participated in the evolution of these fine Cherry Lane Music publications, I'm proud to present this exciting series of books.

Enjoy.

Troy Nelson
Editor
GuitarOne magazine

A LETTER FROM STEVE

Teaching guitar lessons long ago, I realized it really takes a major commitment to be a good teacher. I also quickly got to the point where I felt there was too much homework to be done on my own playing, never mind dedicating my time to teaching.

Still, I felt the desire to help young players from time to time by participating in guitar clinics at music stores. Since I never went to a guitar clinic when I was younger, I had no preconceived notions about what to do or say. Over the years, I began to get a very clear idea of the kinds of questions that guitar players had. I also learned some important differences between the real world and imagined careers. Making a living playing music is within the reach of anyone who loves it, provided they keep a grip on reality.

Self-teaching, adjusting to fit the situation, and good people skills are the keys to making it happen. Learning these skills, in addition to technique, seems to be the way to go. That's why my essays have always leaned more toward the philosophy of being a musician rather than just the technique.

As a writer I am a novice, but I feel my goal will have been achieved if a positive thought is illuminated when you read what I've got to say. In the long run, I believe that a musician's quality is equal only to his quality as a person.

I wish you the best,

Steve Morse

Steve Morse is currently the leader of the Steve Morse Band, the Dixie Dregs, and is a member of Deep Purple.

Photo by Randi Anglin

Contents

Breaking the Ice. 6

Plan B. 9

Pros at Work 12

A Little Push 15

Leap of Faith 18

No Fear. 21

Translations 23

You Are How You Hang. 25

Making Accidents Happen. 27

Pass the Ball. 29

Unquotable Quotes. 32

Finding the Time. 34

Better Solos 36

Road View 38

Merci, Marcel. 40

How'd You Do That? 43

"The Number One Killer" 45

Learning Japanese. 47

New Motivation 49

Into the Comfort Zone 52

Driven to Succeed 55

On with the Show 57

A New Worldview 60

Contract? What Contract? 63

Mind Over Gig 66

Ride to Glory 69

The Composer Within 72

Creative Room 75

Speed Bumps 78

Cleaning Up Your Act, Part 1 80

Cleaning Up Your Act, Part 2 82

The Well-Tempered Communicator 85

Opportunities 87

Losing Through Intimidation 89

Influences 91

Maintaining a Positive Point of View 93

Preparing for the Beyond 95

Another World 98

Trial by Fire 100

Band Chemistry 102

There It Is 104

Creating Space 106

Patience? 108

Looking Back 110

Roadies to Glory 112

Can "Live " Survive? 115

Trading Solos 118

Talkin' Trash 121

Contact 123

Getting the Message 125

Breaking the Ice

I guess it goes back to fishing on a lake in the frozen North. You know, breaking the ice. Once you break it, you can get down to the business of fishing in the lake. Until you do break it, there is no way that you're going to get any fish. If you've read my columns before, you can probably guess that I'm going to make some kind of parallel to the music business from this, right? Right.

Okay, let's say that you've got all your equipment sounding good, everyone in your circle of friends says that you should be playing for a living, and you feel that you could do it if you just got the chance. Why hasn't anything happened? First of all, try to think back to the last time that you were able to show someone new how your music sounds. My theory is that anyone looking for work should be looking for it every day without fail. Suppose you adopted that theory and then looked back at all the days that have passed without a "break."

One popular theory is that once you get your "break," you can just relax because you've got it made. I agree, somewhat, that having a break makes it easier to get brief attention for your next effort; however, you still have to come up with the right goods to benefit from that break. But breaking the ice in this context means getting an opportunity to show what you can do. In my experience, I know of so many people that got their break by walking up to someone they didn't know and breaking the ice—coming across as a friendly, approachable, employable person.

The time-honored way of introducing yourself in the straight, 9-to-5 business world is by sending out resumés and watching the cobwebs grow on the phone. But, in fact, even that method works. I'm still looking for the resumé (that I'm sure I put *somewhere*) of a guy that was seeking work as a roadie/technician. I didn't care how many paragraphs were indented or if the resumé would pass a business correspondence course, but I remember my impression of the guy himself. He came up to me in the studio, where the band was working, being careful to wait for a suitable break point. He very clearly, without wasting any time, got to the point, handed me his credentials and mentioned that he'd like to discuss working together if the need ever arose. Now this guy was tactful. Sometimes people equate being pushy with being successful. In some types of work, that may be tolerable. But if someone can't be tactful when they're asking for work, how could you expect them to be tactful if they're dealing with someone on your behalf when they're stressed out on the job?

What about learning another lesson from the way things are done in the real world? Try to notice how much advertising is ongoing. You already know the brand names of the major consumer goods. Why do they keep on advertising? Why do you see advertising for lots of products over and over? Have you ever been influenced to try something after hearing about it more than once? Well, we all can identify with the payoff of persistence. I think there is an absolutely measurable effect from trying more than one time with most everything. What if you only practiced one day? What if billboards were changed every day, and "For Sale" signs could only stay up for 24 hours? I know for a fact that many people have been hired out of a crowd of prospects because they were properly persistent.

Recently, I was impressed by some folks that went pretty far out of their way to break some new ice by playing in front of a new crowd of people. I was doing some gigs with my trio, and was pleasantly surprised by the opening act in Cincinnati. They sounded great, and I told them so after they got backstage. They looked familiar and I quickly learned that they had opened for us before as the duo Pruett and Davis. After the gig, I was amazed to find out that they were going to drive 11 hours back home because they had to get back to their families and normal lives. Normally, we have no idea who the opening bands will be when playing at showclub-type venues, because the local promoters usually fill that spot with their favorite local act that fits the bill. I was curious as to how these guys hooked up the gig, and impressed by the fact that they contacted the promoter themselves and virtually made it happen. Was it worth it for them? The money probably covered expenses at best, but they sold a bunch of CDs that night, won over a bunch of new fans eager for all good music, and the promoter sure thought he got a good deal. And I got another reminder of the benefits of working hard for what you believe. Even though I've done the same kind of thing in my life, I remember always wondering if it was like that for other people.

Later, on that same leg of our tour, we found out that Larry Mitchell was opening with his band. They delivered a great show and also sold a lot of CDs and stuff. I talked with them and found out that they had traveled quite a distance to play this area that was new to them instead of headlining in familiar territory. Larry got the call because of someone in this Midwestern city who had a connection with the club and thought Larry would be perfect. That probably stemmed from some other time when Larry's easygoing personality made a big impression. The logistics of the whole deal would have stopped lesser musicians. I walked away impressed again with the spirit of people who know what they want to do.

Let me backtrack a bit and reiterate that breaking the ice with someone doesn't mean bugging the heck out of them, or stalking them, or making their life miserable. It simply means that you let people know of your availability so that they can choose to act on it or not. The reason I am saying this is because people still think that I can get them signed or get opening acts on with club owners when that is absolutely not possible in almost every case. Nevertheless, I have seen plenty of guys who do not know how things work and make a real nuisance of themselves.

The main point, however, is not to be afraid to break the ice when you really feel it is appropriate. There are two sayings that come to mind—try to find a balance between them: "You only get one chance to make a first impression," meaning when you do put yourself up for consideration you should be as ready as possible; and "Nothing ventured, nothing gained." I think that one is really the whole point. Good luck in everything.

Plan B

An interesting question that I recently got was, "How far do you go with a project that's having no success before you give up?" To me, the short, idealistic answer is that you don't give up on something that you feel you must do. But there does come a time when you've got to face the facts and admit that there's something wrong. Let's talk about some examples that we've probably all seen in the music business.

Say you've got a group together and there just doesn't seem to be any growth of interest or positive feedback from the live shows. Should you give up and quit the business? Maybe the first thing to do is look at what is weakest about the live show and simply try to change and improve it. I say this over and over, but so many of us just can't bear to fix specific problems; instead we just lament over the effects of the problem. In this case it could be something as simple as getting a better sound mix, or putting an earplug in the singer's ear so he won't sing out of tune. Another thing that might be preventing interest in your band's sound is the material. Maybe a different combination of people writing the tunes would yield something that people would like to listen to.

The first step in fixing a problem seems to be identifying that problem. This is always easier for someone outside to notice, especially in the example of a band. Successful entertainers are almost always interested in what other people think of their act. When they seem like they're not interested, it's usually part of a disinterested image they're trying to cultivate. In any case, having someone you trust come over and check out the sound of your band is a good habit to develop. I say "habit" because you should keep up that kind of attitude of asking for opinions-not necessarily acting on these opinions, but finding out what they are for your arsenal of facts.

Say you've gotten someone in the recording business to check out the band, and they say that everything sounds out of tune, they can't hear the words to the songs, and it just sounds like a bunch of noise. Time to give up? No way. Any band will sound bad if the instruments are out of tune. First, check the tuning and bridge adjustments on the guitars. If they're all right, don't forget the fact that many players push down so hard on the frets that they pull the notes way sharp; also true when strumming really hard on the open strings. Most people who use light strings on the bottom of the guitar need to tune a few cents flat (especially on the low E string) in order to get in tune when they're going at it. Finding this point will take some finesse or at least some trial and error. Also remember that many keyboard presets are just plain out of tune but can be edited to where the average pitch is in the right range.

Your objective listener can't hear the words? It may sound way too obvious, but try cutting down the P.A. distortion by reducing the input level, and adding headroom and volume with more power. You'd be surprised how many people will run a P.A. with the power amps turned down and the input overloading, which gives a lot of unnecessary distortion. Have the singer learn to work the mike: that is, move closer or farther away in order to control the dynamics by himself. A common problem is that the band is too loud for the amount of P.A. that they are using. It's very uncommon to find band members turning down to fit those around them, so try that also. Another one of the possible reasons for the listener saying that it all sounded like noise is that the cymbals may be too much for the small, hard-surfaced room in which that you rehearse. Since it's pretty hard to turn down cymbals, and somewhat difficult to turn down the acoustic drums, try deadening the room or not crashing those cymbals all the time.

So, you can see that none of these suggestions would be such a big deal. There is seldom a reason to call the whole thing off. Let's look at a more difficult example. Joe plays way out of time quite often; you want to get rid of him and get somebody else, but Joe is a good guy and really has his heart in the band. What to do? I would say to tell him nicely but very straight that his timing is a problem that needs serious attention. Chances are good that Joe will start practicing with a mechanical timekeeper right away if his heart really is in the band. Not everyone has the same amount of talent, but it is amazing what a motivated person can accomplish. It's simply your job to either motivate Joe or find someone else.

Motivation and intent are two of the areas that can fall into my category of Hopeless Causes. If someone has zero motivation, you probably should fix the problem by moving on to someone else who does have it. Also, people with plain old bad intentions are usually not going to change their way of looking at things. These are two examples of things that I personally will walk away from, but I should point out that I believe anything can be fixed or modified with enough effort. It's just a question of degree. My personal rule of thumb with people is that those with their heart in what they're doing are worth the effort.

An analogy that could sum up the idea of this column is that the best bands start a new song with maybe a single riff. The riff gets tried by the whole band and everyone experiments with ideas while they're first trying it, and it doesn't sound like anything great to someone who might be listening in. The only difference between that great band and any other is that they will spend less time weeding out the bad ideas and will steer each other to develop good ideas. That comes easily, with experience.

So if something isn't clicking and you feel like giving up, you're in great company; that's the starting point of nearly every band. Just go to Plan B: identify and fix the problem.

Pros at Work

At the summer NAMM show a few months ago, I got the opportunity to play a full two-show night with some great players: Albert Lee and Steve Lukather on guitars, Sherwood Ball and Rodney Crowell on vocals and guitars, Sterling Ball and Dave LaRue on bass, Jimmy Cox on keyboard, and John Ferraro on drums. The theme of the shows was to have a good time, and everyone did. Along the way, some good points to remember came up from watching these pros at work.

I have mentioned it before, but this is one of the important characteristics to have as a musician: the ability to let others be heard, to lend assistance. You've seen it happen in every team sport, but you may not have noticed it as it happened. I'm talking about the people that support the one in the spotlight, the ones who make it possible for the person in the center of the camera shot to shine their best. It's kind of a cliché, but it's true that the guy running the touchdown—to the cheering of the stadium—only got there because of the good blocking and setup by the others on the team. Maybe it's just because I'm often in both the roles of soloist and accompanist, but I absolutely admire folks who can support other musicians on stage. It's not just because there's a skill and an art to doing it, but because it shows that they consider the other musicians worthy of support.

Okay, so we know how to block someone during a football play, but how exactly would you go about supporting a musician who's taking a lead line or a solo? First of all, every situation is somewhat different, so I will have to generalize a bit. On stage that night at NAMM, we had a lot of guitarists at one time, so the most natural way to lend team support was often to stop playing or play very sparsely, at a reduced volume. Along the way, if a solo happened to be building, and if the soloist had some volume left to build with, it might have been appropriate to follow along and help create that buildup underneath. Most musicians naturally play louder than they realize within a group; likewise, most guitarists play too much or too loud when they are backing up another player. Yes, I know, it's all a matter of opinion; but ask the people trying to make themselves heard if they agree with me.

Having said all this, let me say that I was very impressed that night. All the musicians did a wonderful job of backing each other up. I expect it all the time from the guys in this group, but I especially learned a lot about the guest guitarist, Steve Lukather. I'm going to talk about his playing to illustrate some of my points, since I know that none of you will tell him that I was talking about him, right?

The first thing I noticed was that he used the same amps that we were all supplied with, and was smart enough to bring along a few pedals of his own-including an overdrive pedal, which helps when an amp doesn't get a familiar overdrive sound. I felt like Homer Simpson hitting my forehead with the palm of my hand when I realized that I had forgotten to think of that. Next, he was quickly set up, in tune and patient, without any superstar attitude, through a very long sound check. When it came time to play, he laid back on his volume until he knew the form of the sections, then would play very confidently (without overplaying) when a section needed some more support.

It was his soloing that got everyone's attention, mostly because he was able to combine a very melodic approach with a very complete technique, but all at the appropriate times. Usually when I jam with great guitarists, it's a challenge to listen as a fan while keeping the music in mind, because they often show me some very interesting things about the way they play rhythm guitar. This is the best part of my job, being able to occasionally work around guys of this caliber, and it is a real inspiration. Like I said, the whole band is incredible, so I'd like to tour the whole group briefly to show some of the qualities that I think are important.

Albert starts off the tune with a Chuck Berry-style riff that really sets the mood, because he's taking care to relax enough to let the part swing a little instead of attacking it. Sterling comes in with a simple bass part, but it fits perfectly and even has a neat variation that answers each vocal phrase, which I gladly pick up on and follow. Albert and Sherwood both sing in time, in tune, and just make it seem so easy because every phrase feels right. On this tune, Sherwood doesn't take a guitar solo but lays back to let the others be heard. He also turns toward Luke to offer him a clue when the arrangement has a slight surprise ahead, cueing him subtly and clearly. Luke doesn't seem to need much help, since he can somehow predict the future and always seems to know what to do, and he plays a fantastic solo. Albert nods toward Jimmy on the keys for a solo, and we all come down a big notch since the keys don't sound very loud on stage or out front. Jimmy has left a little bit of volume in reserve on the piano sound, and he plays the most convincing piano solo that we've heard in a long time before bringing his volume back down to where it was in order to accompany the song.

John gives us gentle reminders with his drumming if we even think about rushing near the solo trades at the end. He somehow directs the dynamics of the band as a whole, all the while playing this shuffling backbeat with lots of subtle ghosted notes to make it swing even more. Albert comes back for an extended solo that reminds everyone why he's incomparable, and then hands it over to me. Life is tough, but playing with a group like this to back you up isn't, so even I manage to feel good about life after finishing my bit. Rodney does a guest singing spot that shows him to be a natural bandleader with a relaxed confidence that just adds to a powerful feel on the tunes he calls. He keeps his volume on the guitar way down and hands over all the solos to the others. Like the other singers, his voice is great and has absolutely no trace of hesitation or lack of commitment to the songs. Dave comes up and does a guest appearance with me, after literally supporting me during the soundcheck with equipment problems and helping solve an amp problem that Sterling came across. Dave, as usual, plays flawlessly and does the most difficult parts just to give me a broader backup for the music.

I just wanted to let you in on what things stand out to me when I stop and think about working with the pros. The players who support the music are the ones to admire.

A Little Push

I just got back yesterday from another trip on the road that involved lots of gigs and a few guitar clinics. While at the clinics and talking after the shows, I get an idea of what people are concerned about. One of the most frequently asked questions is, "What's the best way to improve my playing?" Obviously, you could spend a lifetime answering questions like that, but I'd like to talk about just one of the best ways to improve your playing.

I suggest that everyone give themselves a goal that forces improvement. What if you had to perform somewhere, in some kind of way, once each week? If you cared about how you sounded, it would be a sure bet that you'd work a little harder than usual with a gig coming up, say, every Saturday. The "performance" could be as simple as inviting friends to listen to the new song you wrote, or working on some new melodic concepts for the weekend jam session.

Maybe you're thinking that this is not necessary, that you would always improve yourself without any prodding or pushing. Let's look at that concept for a bit. Most everyone with a high-school diploma can do basic reading, writing and arithmetic. Do you think that if everyone had only been told, "You need to know these things to work in the real world," that the skills would have been studied nearly as hard? I think it was the thought of a surprise quiz, or the grading of homework, or final exam results, that made most people even consider opening their books on a regular basis. For some people, the biggest efforts were made because of direct competition-which is a type of performance, since it involves scrutiny and comparison. Most everyone can be made to try a little harder in the face of competition, although that is a pretty stressful way to lead your whole life.

Olympic athletes seem to always reach peak form sometime near the Olympic games, simply because they are training for that test or performance, and partly because there are many associated trials and contests beforehand. I like one aspect of athletic training that really fits with the spirit of a performing musician: hitting your personal best. If an Olympic athlete goes all out and doesn't bring home the gold, but does make his or her personal best score, then there can never be a moment of remorse or disgrace. A musician can put out his or her best effort and still be rejected by the record company, or passed over in an audition, or have the publishing house say "No deal." Nobody can predict another's musical tastes, so there is no disgrace with honest effort.

How do you now if you have given your best effort? You need a benchmark, and that should be your past efforts, put in proper perspective. If you've played well in front of your friends and then get a chance to play in front of a spotlight for a crowd of strangers, you can't expect the exact same results, but you sure will benefit from any kind of performance experience you have had.

I think for players that want to perform, there is no substitute for regular performances. A fact about guitar players is that we all think that whatever we play in our practice environment will be similar onstage. While some things can be even easier onstage with experience, it is just plain difficult to be as relaxed and under control when you're playing for others, especially if you're new at it. Picture this: a guy who can play great in his room finally does his first gig in front of people for an audition. He tries to relax, but everything is foreign: he's not used to following other people's timing, he can't hear himself as well as at home, he sees an audience looking at him, etc. The net result is that this guy gave a valiant effort but sounded stiff and had no feel. Someone else gets the gig. Our musician now feels like a failure, but doesn't realize that he did as well as he could expect by even allowing himself to get in front of that much pressure. So in fact he took on an enormous challenge, but instead of feeling good about that much of it, he feels like a failure because he didn't play nearly as well as he does on his own couch.

In this case, taking on too much responsibility at once proved disastrous. The idea I want to promote is to seek out regular but attainable challenges in the form of performances. Imagine that you're given the opportunity to audition for that same gig I described above, but you've taken my advice and have played for anyone that would listen for the last year. Your inner dialogue might be more like this:

"Boy, I sure am nervous. Lots of people here, and I've never met these guys in the band before. Actually, though, that one time I played at my uncle's weekend car sale on a flatbed truck, there were probably just as many people, but since they were scattered all across the car lot, they didn't seem as many. In fact, I have even jammed with quite a few people that I've never met before, whenever my friends and I would rent that rehearsal space in the city's music center. It's not so bad at all, playing with strangers. I remember from the last stage gig I did that feeling a little nervous is normal—I need to remember not to rush and to stay focused on the music. I've carried my equipment to different places to play lots of times, and I expect that it will sound unusual when I first plug in, but I'll relax and get comfortable by knowing that I'm playing the same amp and guitar as I always do in a live situation."

And afterwards . . . "That was fun. Even though I made a few mistakes, I gave it a good shot. Hey, what do you know—I think I got the gig!"

My point is that if you regularly test yourself, you can go back and work on the problems, looking forward to the next time you get to play. Challenge yourself. If you can't find a gig, go up to 10 people you know and invite them over next weekend to hear you play. Buy some drinks and pizza and you'll have an audience, at least till the food's gone. If you want to play, just give yourself a push and do it. Good luck!

Leap of Faith

Sometimes we have to jump. That is, sometimes progress requires a "leap of faith." I'm talking about getting things started, finding new ways of solving problems, and making your presence known.

As usual, I'll use a real-life scenario to relate my point. Joe finally gets a distribution offer for his self-produced album which he's only sold locally. The deal involves a contract, so Joe wisely gets an attorney to look over the contract and negotiate it further. Joe is amazed to find out that the deal is full of language that protects the distributor, and there are only a few sentences saying what the distributor will do for him. Joe asks his lawyer to change the deal to make it more fair. Joe's lawyer comes back and says it's this way or no way—the deal is just not important enough to the other party to warrant making a bunch of changes. Joe knows that there are no other offers from anywhere else, but he just doesn't like giving away anything on paper, even if it's just for this album. What to do?

I hate signing my life away too, but sometimes it's the only way to get others to help you. Let me stress that in this example the contract was limited, was checked over by a pro, and it allowed new possibilities in Joe's career. If the numbers were fair, if the company was as reputable as they come these days, and if there was a way out in case of poor performance by the distributor, I would think that it's time to go for it. Obviously, the idea is to sign away as little as possible, but if that's what it takes to get the ball rolling, just try to retain as many rights as you can and then move forward.

If Joe signs, he might sell a decent number of records and learn a lot more about the record business. If he doesn't sign and never trusts anyone to help him, he can be pretty sure he'll stay exactly where he is. By the way, that's probably where a good number of folks should stay. Not everyone is cut out for the "dive in and take your chances" lifestyle of the music business. Let's look at another example.

Marty's new band has been getting gigs off and on, and this guy comes up and says that he wants to be their manager. He hands them a contract and asks them to sign it. After checking with an attorney, the other guys in the band want to sign it because they remember all the good things the manager told them would happen. In this case, the attorney has no idea of how good the manager is, only that the contract language is "industry standard" and therefore acceptable, in his opinion. Marty, however, is skeptical since the manager has no real track record of success. Neither does the band, of course.

In this case, it might be wise to have a trial period or maybe an agreement that the manager only gets a commission for income that is a direct result of his work. My motto is to never consider signing unless you get something significant for it. If someone wants to be your manager, I say let them prove themselves, perhaps in a limited time frame.

In this case, Marty did the talking and the manager agreed to work for a year with no contract, but the band agreed to give up a commission for every gig they played during the time that they were satisfied with the manager. When the band was lucky enough to get signed and have a big record, they kept the same manager but always refused to sign any long-term commitment with him. The reason? The manager had no risk; he had made no real investment to justify a long-term contract. When a record company puts up money to record and promote a band, they demand a long-term contract to assure the best chance of making back a profit. When a manager puts up a lot of his own money up front, maybe then he can demand the same, but most deals should be based on performance and fair reward.

How about musical leaps of faith? Picture this scene at rehearsal: everyone is arguing about whether they should try this new tune at the gig this weekend. Everyone's unsure about how well the audience will like it. To me, there's no way around it—you have to play the new tune out to give it a fair chance. How else will you find out? If you only play stuff that you know everyone will like, then you're already filtering out possibilities that you'll never know about.

How about the people that help out with a band? Once someone has proven that they are responsible and can be trusted, then by all means, take advantage of the opportunity to have some help (it may even allow you to spend more time on the music). Give them important tasks and try never to take away their responsibility or authority unless absolutely necessary. For example, Big John always wanted to be a roadie and was always hanging out with the band and helping load and drive the van. The band started paying him to set up and tear down every gig. Big John loved it and he was really on the ball. He even did some advance checking on this big opening-act slot that the band had coming up. Big John found out that the equipment needed to get on and off the stage quickly, since there were three different bands with a tight schedule. He asked the band to hire an extra helper for the gig. The band had never played a gig like that and didn't understand the need to spend any more money on that night, so they told him no.

Now here was Big John, who had earned their trust by hauling their equipment at every gig up till now, but he suddenly couldn't be trusted to do the right thing at an important show. Basically, the band had taken away his authority and part of his self-esteem, the real payoffs for most people doing jobs they actually care about. Now, let's imagine the band had said, "Big John, whatever you think is best. You've always done right by us." The gig happens, the band is offstage on schedule, and the promoter compliments them on their professional performance and inquires about upcoming opening spots for the band. Oh yeah, and Big John feels like he would do anything for this band since they believed in him and trusted him.

Be informed enough to make intelligent decisions, and then have a little faith. You know the old saying, "Look before you leap?" It's not "Look before you procrastinate forever and wither away and die." Seriously—if it's your vision, make it happen.

No Fear

I have always seen that "No Fear" sticker on the back of custom trucks and all sorts of vehicles and wondered if it was a message that the drivers were trying to believe, or just some sticker that they bought because it was cool at the time. Regardless, everybody thinks that it's really easy to face everything with no fear, until it's their turn to be in unfamiliar territory. Let's face it, if we all had less fear of the unknown, there would be a huge increase in creativity and productivity as we all decided to try new approaches, take on new challenges, and try something other than the most obvious or traditional solution. Anyway, lots of folks have asked me if I ever get scared before a gig. I've always thought that I will always have some excitement before every gig because of the unknown elements of improvisation, performance, and the genuine desire to please the audience. Most people will admit to "a state of heightened awareness," or something like that, but every red-blooded musician is at least a little nervous when truly facing the unknown.

I just had a huge lesson in how useful facing the unknown can be. For over a year I knew that I was supposed to do this Guitar Summit concert for a proper sit-down-and-listen, fine-arts-performance-type audience. I got to make new friends and learn something from Jorma Kaukonen, Kenny Burrell, and Manuel Barrueco. Each had a distinctive style and influences, and that's what made the show interesting. The first night, I heard them all play and I wasn't too sure how my mixture of styles would work with the audience. I was actually sitting there worrying about it when I realized that there is only one way to find out. In truth, I was a little nervous about the unknown until I thought about that "No Fear" sticker. It made me chuckle that I was now basing my mental balance on some bumper sticker that I saw at a red light in traffic. Anyway, it turned out to be good advice.

We all played together at the end on an arrangement brought in by Kenny Burrell. It started with Manuel playing a straight Bach lute piece. From this evolved a melody, and then improvisations were placed over that harmonic progression. We only had a short time at the hotel to go over it, but Kenny was absolutely sure that everyone should play it his own way and be free to improvise with very little coaching from him. That seemed like a tremendous leap of faith to me, since he could have shortened or simplified the arrangement and drilled it into everybody, but instead he wanted something to be unique about every performance. Let me tell you, this was exciting to realize that one the masters of jazz guitar trusted us enough to leave it at that. And it worked. "King Kenny" is what I nicknamed him after that. What else could I call a guy who's been there, done that before I knew what a guitar was, and is still playing like a master? Oh yeah, and who took the time to bring us all together on that piece?

All I knew about Jorma before the gig was that I had learned one of his Jefferson Airplane acoustic pieces way back when. I also knew that the Dregs were going to play a gig with him the day our friend and road manager, Twiggs, died in front of us in a parachuting accident. Needless to say, we didn't make that gig, and I never met Jorma. Fifteen years later, here I am realizing that I really like this guy, and discovering that a number of acoustic pieces I recognized and could remember were played by him. Jorma had no fear. This guy just walked up and played his heart out. Hardly said a word, just dug in and went for it. By the time he finished his set, I hadn't gone on yet, but I realized how much the man showed me about playing straight from the heart. I was feeling better still.

Manuel was a scary player, because he had serious classical technique, but an amazing musicality. I remember wondering why it's so easy for guys like him, then I realized that everybody practices, plays, and improves. I was surprised to hear him say that he also felt nervous about his performance at first. I couldn't detect a trace. Since I was going on after Manuel with an electric classical guitar in front of an audience who just heard a virtuoso classical guitarist, you can appreciate how weird it was for me to walk on stage.

After the polite applause for just walking out, I plugged in and checked my tuning, and you really could have heard a pin drop. A sea of dark silhouettes, totally silent, sure to hear my every mistake or hesitation. I self-consciously adjusted the knobs on my direct box to the P.A. rig. I remember wishing that I had a pin I could actually drop. It was time to review the lessons I had learned that day. Even Manuel had wondered how he would be received, so quit worrying about that, the people out there just want to see some genuine, passionate music, I thought. Jorma proved that playing from your heart and letting the music tell the story was very successful. Part of my set was improvisation, and King Kenny had just given me a big lesson on loosening up and improvising better, using as inspiration his melodic, ever changing, no-problem solos. Once again, I realized that we all get a little nervous before each show, or else we wouldn't care. I've been on stage a lot of my life, and solo playing is as intense as it gets, but I did relax and felt that surge of strength that can only come when you realize you're going to share something you really believe in with the audience. If the music's inside, you should give it a try. No fear.

Translations

We've all read articles that begin with a definition of a word from Webster's Dictionary, but something tells me that Webster never spent much time on the road. So I will attempt to give some common music-business phrases some translation.

Record Contract Imminent Usually this phrase is found after "Guitarist Wanted" on a bulletin board. It means that after they get a guitarist there will be almost enough people to actually begin rehearsals for their first gig ever.

Trust me This is what people who don't create music tell you after they've convinced you to make some kind of uncomfortable change to your music. It translates to a common phrase that can't be printed in this magazine.

Net Royalties Fictitious term used in record contracts—no such thing for artists that don't hit high chart numbers.

Indemnify What you do when you sign 80 pages of legalese that say it's all your fault if they don't make a lot of money off of you.

Discover What they did to you when you make them a lot of money.

Recoupable Expense A term used to describe why there are no Net Royalties.

Negotiating the Contract A process that's basically done in five minutes when the head of Legal Affairs asks the president of the label what amount he's going to sign the band for. It then takes corporate lawyers weeks to commit it to paper.

I got it in one take I got it after spending all day in the studio.

2 p.m. rehearsal 4 p.m. rehearsal.

Hey guys, I'll be back to finish practicing after I get some pizza See you tomorrow.

That guy can only play fast and he has no emotion I can't play fast.

That guy is totally boring I wish I could get my guitar to sound like that.

We can make it to the next gig by morning We can make it to the first gas stop by morning since it'll take forever to get everyone in the vehicle.

Last night I had to drive the whole way myself It was a 50-mile trip.

Hey guys, I figure it's time we started playing some of my songs, too! I'll be fired shortly.

It's only five sets each night. No problem. The last guitarist in the band went nuts.

The record is selling well (This is the only music-business phrase that does not require translation.)

If you don't think I'm doing such a great job managing your career, then just go get someone else! If you read your contract carefully, you'll see that I've got you by the balls.

The soundboard just crapped out on me the reason your mic was off is because I forgot to un-mute it.

It'll sound a lot better when the people come in Soundcheck is over.

The club owner said he'd have a ride for us to go back to our rooms Call a cab.

The club owner said we had a good night and he wants us back The club owner must be new in the business.

The club owner said he lost money, but he wants us to come back on the next trip The club owner made good money and is not new to the business.

It's a routing date. It's right on the way to your next gig It's going to pay less than your expenses for that day.

It's a career date. It's great exposure You're playing for free.

It's the hottest club in town. There's always record-company people there checking out new bands You're going to pay to play.

You'll be playing for a percentage of the door Keep the guest list down to a reasonable number so you can buy gas to get home.

Improvising When you find a way to fit all your equipment in your mom's car after your van breaks down.

Special Thanks What musicians give when they realize they're speaking the only universal language.

You Are How You Hang

I've seen it too many times to think that it's just a coincidence. I'm convinced that people who do outstanding things got to be that way as a result of circumstances they created themselves. Yes, I know, there must be some amount of genetic influence, but I'm going to have to go with environment as the strongest influence, at least concerning the people I've met.

I contend that the poor kid who lives in a rundown part of town with crime everywhere can have a positive environment somewhere. Obviously, I have to make the other illustration that the wealthy family may not be giving the impressionable kid they brought into this world a healthy environment for growth just because they live in a nicely manicured neighborhood.

Who cares? I'll say it again, differently. All the great guitarists I've gotten to know had some strong positive influence in their lives. The ones who had more positive influence tend to be consistently productive without falling into the various pits of vice and hopelessness. I think it's more important than just about anything else that you learn how to analyze and fix problems, in life and in music.

If you're still about to flip the page and read something else, think about this. A guy who stays five minutes after quitting time to take care of a problem, instead of bolting out the door, is going to be the same guy who tries just one more time to figure out the mystery note on the solo he's trying to learn from a record. The girl who goes out of her way to help someone with a solution at work might be the singer who manages to get the rest of the band interested in finding a better bridge for that new tune.

We've all seen how our environment changes us. Once people get in a more crowded, impersonal environment, they are less inclined to care what other people think and are more rude. Those same people could walk in a place of worship filled with quiet people, and they too will be quiet. Now imagine what it would be like if the people you are working with were constantly bummed out and saying that everything's just a waste of time and there's no use trying. Is that going to give you much incentive to go the extra mile? Of course not. In that type of scenario, the common denominator is just too low to prompt growth.

Everything we do in our lives affects the way we play our guitars. Really. If you've got to have a day job to support your musical habit, make it count. How? By making sure you are hanging around with people you can admire and respect. The title of this column says what I mean: the people you hang out with will end up influencing the way you think. The way you think is definitely connected to whether or not you will improve your playing.

Alright, let's look at an example. Say you've got a chance to do a day gig for seven dollars an hour, but you have to work with a sleazy bunch of con artists. On the other hand, you know this great family restaurant that has stood the test of time because of great atmosphere and service., but it's going to be five dollars an hour plus food. What should you do? The only reason it's going to be a tough decision is that it's hard to live on five dollars an hour, though that big free meal once a day will help. You see, there really is no way you could take the sleazy job, because it would kill part of what makes you motivated to make music. Being around a pleasant, hard-working group of people doing a good job will help offset the fact that you can't be working on your music during the day. If you keep alert at the job, you will definitely learn good work habits and people skills from the folks who have built their business on those things. Good work habits and people skills are golden assets for anything you do in life.

Another example. Joe is a dirtbag. But his band has an opening for a guitarist to start right away playing five sets a night, six nights a week. Everyone knows that the onstage vibe with this band really blows, but you are interested in that $250 a week. The only other choice you see is an opportunity to work on a duo with an incredibly talented keyboard player, but you will probably only work around three nights a week for $75 a pop. What to do? Another no-brainer. Obviously, the first gig will suck the life out of you in no time because of the vibe and the repetition. The duo gig is a much better deal just because you will be so much more inspired by the company you'll be keeping on the job, plus the fact that there will be several nights a week to go to other jam sessions or take some extra classes at the music school.

Everything you do is an opportunity to shape your future. You can pretty much be what you choose to be.

Making Accidents Happen

"Watch out, you'll put your eye out with that!" Everybody's always trying to make sure you never have an accident, right? Well, one of the best ways to create new music is to establish an environment that allows you to make good use of "musical accidents." Think about it: If you try something new and it really is unlike anything that you've ever done, it won't be familiar or comfortable. Certainly, if you play something that is comfortable, it can be useable and worth keeping, but let's talk about something different: the idea of new, unfamiliar musical or technical discoveries.

First of all, I think it's possible to lead a perfectly happy life without being forced to make astounding new discoveries. And we know that it's possible to be a very useful musician without doing much creating at all. In fact, I believe that musicians who are considered creative actually spend a very small amount of time discovering and navigating totally unfamiliar territory. However . . .

The musicians that seem to be the most sought-after, the ones with whom most people want to work, are usually creative. Those guitarists that have their own sound and identity obviously have done at least one thing different from everyone else in order to get that sound. You have to be open to creativity and the possibility of different things happening. It is easy to get a creative state of mind going, and once you do, it will help everything you do.

Now, I also have to warn you of some of the drawbacks of establishing a creative mindset. For one thing, you will start seeing creative possibilities in every situation, but you may not have the means to actualize your ideas. You might be waiting in line at some inefficient bureaucratic agency when your mind starts coming up with a thousand ways to run the process more efficiently; meanwhile, you're better off just standing there and taking it. Another drawback might be when someone says, "Just give me one good reason why I should do that"—and you can give them a reason. Suddenly you've got an opinion on everything. It's a drawback of having a creative outlook.

But the good things that occur will be the direct result of seeing new possibilities. And the good things totally outweigh the bad. Still, what does this all have to do with accidents? I'm talking about harmless and artistic accidents that lead to new and useful ideas. Unplanned creativity. To achieve this, I think the first step is to allow yourself enough freedom to crash and burn if you get too close to the edge. Does that mean that you should get wasted at a gig and explore the outer edges of sanity, or attempt other such feats? Well, obviously, you will want to explore new and perhaps radical stuff away from the public until you are sure that doing it during a performance is a positive experience. But a clear mind will always get more from your brain's creativity and allow you the chance to remember how you got where you did.

The second step is to create a physical environment for creative accidents. It may be as simple as sitting in your room with no distractions. Or it might be more involved, like finding a few other musicians who are fun to jam with and rounding up a good place to get together. One tool that really helps take some pressure off of being purposely creative is a good tape machine. You should leave it running the whole time you're working on ideas; that way you know you can always go back and find any interesting bits that you might have come up with unexpectedly. I imagine that a hard-disk recorder would be great for this, since you could instantly go back to an approximate time, find the part you like, and save it without keeping the other not-so-great stuff. In the absence of such cool technology, though, you could use a $30 boombox that has two cassette decks in it, and bounce the good ideas onto another tape. Every serious writing session I've observed or been a part of has included some means to record the idea once it is considered to be worth a second look or listen. Many ideas can be found by listening back to spontaneous jams.

There's even an art to identifying a useable idea, because many times you'll come across a diamond in the rough. Open your mind to new ideas when you shift to creative mode, and you'll catch more possible starting points. In order to capitalize on your discoveries, you'll have to develop a habit of pursuing them further, rather than just saying, "That was a neat idea. Oh well, let's go watch TV now." In this option-overloaded world in which we live, it's not enough to just have the raw ideas—you have to put everything together in order to really experience some gain. Still, new creations do require the raw material, no matter what. So why not try to go into your next practice session with at least some time reserved for letting accidents happen?

Pass the Ball

The main thing I remember about watching my first professional basketball game in person was that some of the slickest moves were people simply passing the ball, not those sports-highlights type of slam-dunk shots shown on the news. In sports, as in music, the best players are "team" players.

Most everyone likes to be around the type of people who can involve others in conversation and other activities that are going on. Studies always show that those who tend to dominate conversations are seen as less interesting to talk with than those who allow equal time for everyone. Common sense tells you that the same goes in music. That should be reason enough to think about how you can support others musically. In the ballgame analogy, the chances of scoring are much better when variety is introduced into the playing strategy. Plus, when one of the athletes suddenly passes the ball to another player, it adds that element of surprise. Let's face it: To be a valuable player, you've got to learn to support others. So what's the problem? I'll give you some examples.

Jim has just finished his guitar solo and the keyboard-featured theme is coming up next, but Jim is still wailing away at full bore, maybe thinking that it's the soundman's problem. Meanwhile, the keyboard player is going over that joke in his mind: Q: How do you get a guitarist to turn down? A: Put some sheet music in front of him. In reality, the keyboard player doesn't realize that there are some unique problems facing guitarists who use amp distortion as part of their sound.

The first is volume control. When the front end of an amp is overloaded or overdriven, the signal naturally gets compressed to some extent, with the result that turning down the guitar won't reduce the volume until that level of overdrive has been passed. Used in conjunction with a typical tube amp's overdrive channel, your guitar's volume level controls the characteristics of the distortion: with the guitar on 10, you'll get that familiar fat, driven sound; on 8, the thickness but not the volume is reduced; 6 thins the sound to the point that if you pick softly it sounds clean; 5 is clean with some volume reduction; 3 is significantly softer with some obvious loss of high-end. It all varies, of course, with factors like the amount of overdrive set on the amp and the audio taper of your volume pot, but generally you don't get to the point that the guitar is turning down until you reach somewhere between 5 and 6. Then half of the pot's rotation brings the vol-ume to zero, giving a much smaller target if you want a specific volume reduction. (By the way, this same scenario can happen with a clean sound when you run through a compressor.)

Solutions? To me, the best solution is to be able to change volume, so try putting a volume pedal in your effects loop to act as a master volume control. Or, if you have an effects loop bypass switch, you could have an electronically adept friend put a trim pot in a box that goes in your effects looop. Then, when you bypass the loop you're at your selected volume, but when you switch on the loop you're at a reduced master volume level determined by the trim pot. The advantage is that the volume reduction will always be the same, at the tap of a switch. For a few cents you could even modify a guitar cord by putting a resistor across it and plugging it from Send to Return in the loop, but you would have to experiment to find the right value resistor. A more ungainly solution, but one that sounds better because the power tubes would be worked at the same level all the time, is to switch in a power attenuator that diverts some of the energy away from the speakers, or even switch off some speakers in such a way that the impedance to the amp doesn't change. I've tried these ideas, and they are complicated, but they work. Just remember that reducing the number of speakers doesn't help as much if you're being miked.

What about switching to a whole other amp rig at a different volume and sound? Plenty of people use that technique, and one neat variation is to plug your guitar into a panning pedal so that you can slowly change from one sound to the other. If you play through a dedicated preamp into a power amp, just put a volume pedal after the preamp and you won't have to touch the effect sends. You might try some different pots in the pedal to give a smoother reduction in volume. It's also possible that simply using channel switching will give you the results you want.

Other techniques for volume change are possible with no change in the amp sound. One way to lower apparent volume is to reduce the length and density of what you're playing. As you might know, muting the strings with your picking hand while you're playing does sound cool, and reduce the length of the notes, but it also allows a distorting amp to give an exaggerated low-end response. Turn down the volume pot on the guitar a few numbers to minimize the problem. There's quite a bit of art involved in changing the density, and it warrants a very long discussion, but the essence of the idea is to play less when someone else is trying to be heard, and fill in the gaps if you want to keep the illusion that you're playing constantly. Another way to help someone be heard is to stay well below them in pitch. If they're playing in a middle register, only play the bottom note of the chords, leaving out the notes that would be close enough in pitch to interfere.

I'm going to summarize by saying that the most important technique in allowing others to be heard is to simply have the desire to hear them. Then you'll do all these things more naturally.

Unquotable Quotes

A lot of people who read my article on music-business translations have asked me for some more. Like the last bunch, these are pretty much based on reality rather than literal interpretation. Yes, it's possible that they might seem just the tiniest bit cynical, but they've stood the test of time.

They said the gig was right around here. I don't have a map or directions.

No big deal, it's just a two-hour drive. From well past the starting point of the drive to the point where you start seeing signs telling you how many more miles it is to the destination city will take 120 minutes of non-stop driving.

I just have a few names for the guest list. I just have 25% of the capacity of the gig to put on the list.

So, I hear you guys are playing in town tonight. How many people can I put on your guest list?

Hey man, long time no see. I was just calling to check in after not talking to you for the last couple years. How many people can I put on your guest list?

Don't hesitate to sign it—this is all standard industry stuff. Your lawyer would never let you sign it if he read it.

This part of the contract is the same for everyone in the business. This part, like all parts, is negotiable.

We're not interested in signing you. I just don't hear any hits on this tape. Three other bands that I rejected are huge, with multiplatinum albums.

I just got one of my bands signed to a million-dollar recording contract. Let's see. . . $5,000 recording budget after 200 album options would be a million bucks.

It felt like you guys were dragging on that last tune. I was rushing.

Let's just try another take. That take was fine, but I think we're supposed to do a lot of takes for some reason.

I don't know, what do you think? Hi, I'm your producer.

Digital just doesn't work for rock and roll. It changes the sound too much. Digital reproduces the sound too much like how you played it.

How can I possibly cut tracks in this studio with a headphone mix like that?! Some of the other musicians were audible in the head-phone mix.

See how much better it sounds when I push up this fader? I'm mov-ing an unused fader and I haven't got a clue.

If you can't make your record on 16 tracks, you shouldn't be in this business! We have only a 16-track machine.

We really like playing more intimate venues. Our 15 minutes of fame is running out and we can't draw a crowd anywhere.

I decided to leave the band because of musical differences. The rea-son they fired me is still not clear.

I must have written at least 50% of every song on the album and I never even got a songwriting credit! Once when I dropped by, they were trying some new material and I said it sounded cool.

Spinal Tap wasn't a funny movie at all. I've lived the entire story.

All musicians are comedians. All musicians want to be comedians.

On a less cynical note, I suggest that the "Thought for the Month" should be to show someone some of what you have learned about playing the guitar. Think about it: At some point there was somebody who gave you some advice or just let you try holding a guitar for the first time, or something that helped fire up your interest. Everyone knows a person who seems fascinated or at least interested in guitar playing. Especially if it's a younger person who looks up to you, take a little time to introduce them to what you know. Make a positive impression on a youngster and we might end up with more musi-cians in the world. Despite the jokes, it would be a better place.

Finding the Time

Actually, this one should be called "More on finding the time" (Moron Finding The Time?), mainly because I've written in the past about ways to find time to get the deed done. The reason I think it's important is because so many people could do incredible things on the guitar if they would only stick with the program for a while. You know, practice the thing. It's one of the most repeated questions whenever I do a guitar seminar: "How long each day do you practice?"

The answer is, of course, "That depends." If I've just played a show and I'm getting ready to go to sleep, I'll probably feel guilty if I don't go over something that felt a little weird during the gig. It may take only a few minutes, or it may lead to a songwriting idea, which always takes precedence over things like sleeping. Or, if I'm finally home on one of those mythical "days off" that I've always heard about, I might only be able to spend an interruption-filled hour or so with the beast, trying to find some inspiration. Normally, though, I'd guess a couple of hours is normal, including occasional interruptions.

One thing I've noticed is that when I'm gearing up to go play some gigs, I really need to practice more than my schedule will easily allow. So, I try some motivational techniques, or mind games, to make sure that I get enough. First of all, I make it easy to begin practicing at the drop of a hat. For me, it's great to have a nice guitar tuned up and ready in one or two rooms of the home, so that I can easily grab it for a "quickie." It's surprising to see how much you can accomplish in 15 minutes of concentration. If you do that four times a day, I guarantee you'll see more progress than from a typical hour-long allotment of practice time.

Don't you think you need to practice more? How about booking a gig at least once every two weeks? When you get on stage and feel like you wish it were as easy to play those solos as it was in your room, remember what it feels like. Later, as you're remembering that feeling of wishing you were better prepared, you'll get to work and make a new practice schedule.

I used to set my alarm a few minutes early while I was going to school, and spent a few minutes in the morning working on memory items like modes or repertoire, or creative but mind-draining work such as analyzing music and then writing variations. I first tried waking up a bit early after my mom pointed out that your mind is very receptive to factual, analytical, and memory-programming items at that time of the day. I tried it and it worked, plus it was no problem to put in a few minutes in the morning. Instead of moving slowly to get ready to walk out the door, I moved faster, and had my 15 minutes right there.

The extra time didn't take the place of a long practice session; it just helped me catch up and move ahead more quickly. Think about this analogy: If it takes 60 horsepower to keep your big American auto moving at the legal speed limit, and you supply just 15 more horsepower to the drive wheels, you will definitely be getting a speeding ticket because every bit of that extra horsepower can be used for acceleration and fighting the aerodynamic drag until it reaches a noticeably higher equilibrium. As you're sitting there waiting to sign the speeding ticket, you can relate this analogy to your playing. In fact, just one more horsepower will see you steadily pull away from someone that you were pacing with the cruise control on.

Okay, so let's say that you believe an extra, small practice session will help, or that you could conceivably break your practicing up into modular sections throughout the day. Still, how do you do it? One other thing would be to have different goals for sections of your day. Maybe it could go like this: *Morning*—15 minutes of reviewing the modes, with a different fingering for each. *After work or school*—30 minutes including an easy warmup, some jamming on your favorite feels, and technique work. *Sometime before bed*—15 quiet minutes listening for the music inside and trying to recreate it on your guitar— you know, creative stuff.

Naturally, everything is easier said than done, but the fact is that if you really start to feel improvement and you love to play the guitar, you will notice that it becomes easier to find those bits of time and that you look forward to them. It's kind of like those health clubs or gyms; the people that could really use them are too intimidated or can't visualize the benefits, but the ones that go regularly see nice results and look forward to their next visit.

Because of this, I think it's important to see regular improvement to reinforce the benefits of steady practice. Also, it's important to have fun with it so that there is always some thrill. Why do so many kids get good at skateboarding but totally hate school? Obviously, one is more fun.

Better Solos

Let's talk about a subject that's important to all guitar players at some point: improving your solos. First of all, I know there are some players out there who say they don't care about soloing and that it's just too self-indulgent, etc., but I think they are in the minority.

What makes a good solo? This also brings up another question: How can music be "good" or "not good"? While I do agree that you can't quantify "goodness" or express it in exact units, we all know when something's great or when something really sucks, right? I'm going to have to assume that you answered yes in order to continue with this column. Okay, so what makes up a good solo? In my opinion, a good solo has some shape, or phrasing, memorable content, and genuine emotion. We'll tackle these concepts one at a time.

Phrasing. I've said it before, and it will always be true that people can handle an amazing amount of individuality in music if there is some semblance of phrasing. You can get away with playing very strange stuff if you really need to, as long as there are some natural breaks in the action. Even if you play recognizable, trendy styles, just putting in natural phrasing will make everyone think you're a genius. As I've mentioned to many people at seminars, if you do nothing else but this, you will be seen as an improved player.

One of the best exercises to practice phrasing is one of the simplest, but hardest for people to remember onstage: Play two-bar phrases. That means every other bar will be the beginning of another phrase. For a basic exercise, try playing a bar and a half of eighth notes and ending the second bar with a half note. In real life, you'll want to change the shape of each phrase so they all don't have exactly the same rhythm. Now try a phrase pattern with the first two-bar phrase the same as the third two-bar phrase. If each letter of the alphabet corresponds to a similar phrase structure, it could be A-B-A-C to make an eight-bar section that seems well thought out. In reality, all you have to do is try to make the third phrase relate to the first and you can be improvising the whole time-which, of course, is the best way to play a solo.

Here's another angle to try. Play the phrases A-B-A-B with regard to rhythm only. Make the second phrase ascending, and the fourth phrase descending. For the most basic example of this concept, make the first and third phrases exactly the same. As you get more experience with practicing this phrasing, you will be able to add interesting changes so that while no two phrases are exactly alike, they will seem to be from a similar concept. The little nuances and changes will help keep the exercise from sounding too much like a nursery rhyme.

Content. This is one of those areas of music that's difficult to describe in words. Let's just say that one ingredient that will always work is melodic phrasing. What is melodic, anyway? It's the quality of balance, surprise, and change that keeps notes from sounding just like scales and arpeggios. Let's try a simple exercise to illustrate some concepts that could contribute to a melodic style. My disclaimer is that it takes more than just a simple exercise to play melodically, but just try to get my point. This exercise will be in four phrases like the last one. Phrase 1 can be a pattern like: 1-2-3-4-3-2-1, ending on the 7th just below 1. Phrase 3 could be similar to Phrase 1. Phrase 4 would go: rest-1-2-3-4-5-7, ending up an octave on 1.

If all those numbers seem too confusing to think about, just look at the exercise like this: pattern, downward line, pattern revisited, upward line. Once again, in real life, nobody is going to be actually sitting there thinking those words, but we practice in order to be free and relaxed in performance. We don't have to practice the same way that we perform. In fact, I believe a certain amount of our practice time should be radically different than performing in order to try new things thoroughly.

Honest emotion. Another tough one to describe, but I think that we can tell when someone really feels it, versus when he's just going through the motions. Imagine that an emotional solo is what you say when you're in a passionate argument about something, and a worked-out solo is a politician reading a prepared speech. Which one has the honest emotion? Try to do everything you can to make your solo come as easily as speech, so that when you are playing, you are really describing a unique moment that can never be duplicated. Think about it: When someone asks you the same question over and over, you eventually get so tired of giving the answer that it can be heard in your vocal expression. Similarly, trying to repeatedly play the same exact ideas in a solo can begin to sound uninspired. To really have honest emotion, you have to jump off the edge and take a chance. If anyone criticizes you for that, they're missing the excitement and involvement of music.

Hopefully, every solo you play will incorporate your lifetime of experience. The best way to acquire a lifetime of experience is to make sure you put something musical into your playing every day.

Since I've been touring quite a bit this year, it seems like a good time to offer some glimpses of things that still amaze, amuse or confound me. In no particular order, here are some examples.

The security guys at the front of the stage in one country violently squelch any overt enthusiasm of the crowd on the floor.

The same type of security guys in another country hand out bottles of water to the sweaty, hot crowd in front. Some people in the crowd are lifted over the barrier for a chance to recover.

In yet another country, an excited fan jumps onstage just to shake hands. He is immediately tackled by an equally excited security guy and gets his head smashed after the both of them slide off the stage and collide with a metal barrier. Later, our singer introduces himself to the now infamous security guy by punching him. The road manager initiates extensive negotiations to avoid legal repercussions.

The last example of this theme: At another extremely hot, crowded concert, security is doing nothing but helping people who are suffering from being squeezed up front. Our singer openly pays tribute to their helpful attitude, and the band and the entire crowd applaud the security team.

A fan proudly presents a CD for us to autograph. It's a bootleg from a show we just played a few weeks ago, with cover artwork, liner notes, and some phony record company name. Bootlegs like this are very common, but this seemed to be manufactured quicker than a label could circulate an interoffice memo about where to have lunch to discuss a live album.

It's summertime and the air conditioning is broken on the band's bus. It's unbearably hot, and it's a really long drive with no windows to open. You don't know what you've got till it's gone.

A typical party on the bus the day of a gig: English rock stars are sitting at the table with an Oxford dictionary on hand, breezing through obscure, cryptic crossword puzzles, sipping tea. Things are somewhat different after the gig, of course.

The opening band starts and ends on time—exactly on time—and are careful to do just what the stage manager tells them. Later they would be surprised to find that the entire headlining band had noticed those things, which made a very favorable impression. It appears that doing your job well counts more than handing out lots of your tapes to people who are not in the business of signing bands to labels.

I discover that I neglected to pack my suitcase to cover outdoor gigs that are absolutely finger-numbing cold and others that are well over 100 degrees onstage. Neither did I pack for the almost-fixed bus air-conditioning, which freezes the windows upstairs but still passes for a sauna downstairs.

After a guitar seminar one afternoon, a huge traffic jam threatens to keep me from getting across town in time for a gig. Spotting the problem in advance, the organizers have a police car waiting for me to ride in. As we begin the drive by rocketing down a one-way street the wrong way, all thoughts turn to survival. Just like in a chase scene from a movie, we drive down sidewalks, into oncoming traffic, jolt across curbs, scatter innocent pedestrians, and marvel at how little attention is paid to the blaring siren and flashing lights of this vehicle. At one point the four-wheel disc/anti-lock brakes just barely keep us from crashing. I really wish I could convey to the driver that it's okay if we just take some back roads and drive normally.

I notice once again that nearly everything that can be bought in the world can be bought for less money in the U.S. After hearing many explanations for this phenomenon, I still don't quite understand the reason. Fuel, food, hotels and musical instruments are things that I can't help but notice in my everyday travels. For the fans, train tickets, gasoline, and the price of admission are all much higher than we're used to in the States. Being away from home for so many weeks makes it easy to understand why so many people elsewhere in the world see the U.S. as a land of opportunity.

Everyone knows the line that music is the universal language, but as we constantly change the nationality of each audience and the opening band, it really does ring true. Yes, another true fact: Music makes people get together and get happy. Maybe we should help it grow in the U.S., since entertainment appears to be one of our only national surplus exports. If someone gives you a hard time about wanting to be in a band and play music for a living, ask them, "How else are we going to bring down our trade deficit?"

Merci, Marcel

Something just happened that caused me to remember this great session to which I was invited in Nashville. I got to play with Albert Lee, Bela Fleck, Buddy Emmons, and a great rhythm section, met Chet Atkins, and was invited to play on three different albums with the best-known guitarist of France, Marcel Dadi.

What made me think about this session was the explosion of the TWA flight to Paris. I heard that Marcel Dadi was on the flight, as well as members of saxophonist Wayne Shorter's family and hundreds of other innocent people. Marcel was one of the nicest guys you could meet in the business and a great guitarist. The fact that he invited me to play on his albums was a big honor, but to me, it showed that he was not afraid to try mixing up styles, or at least images.

The session began with that kind of "I'm not quite sure I belong here" feeling that comes from meeting a healthy challenge. Albert was already a close friend, so I had no problem relaxing around him. The other guys, though, are legends of Nashville history. I remember thinking that Mark O'Connor is also, and I know him well enough to relax and play with, so I should just consider that the rest of the guys are human as well. That line of thinking went fine until we started playing.

Albert took the first solo on the first chart. It defined what a great solo should have: spontaneity, fluid motion, effortless technique, energy, melodic content. This always happens when Albert plays, by the way, so I was merely awestruck instead of comatose. Then Bela Fleck took one, and it was in that top league along with Albert's. The sound was like a banjo, but the lines were more like a mixture of saxophone, vibes, hammered dulcimer, and blues guitar. I had trouble believing that these guys' first takes were this good. I occasionally play a little bit of banjo, and I think this guy is a genius. I'm also an extremely shy, beginner pedal-steel player, and guess who was next? Buddy Emmons hit the downbeat of the third solo in fifth gear, and I swear, it sounded like one of those super-hot moments that mainstream country radio has in a hit song from time to time. It was authentic, smoking, double-time, string pulling, right-in-the-pocket, keeper solo material. I have never seen anything like it from so close, so I was just laughing and totally getting into it as a listener. I guess I was playing some kind of sparse rhythmic thing, and as I remember, there was suddenly an awkward moment where I realized that I was too involved watching the show to catch my solo spot.

So then I was at the end of the track, quickly asking the engineer to rewind to bar 128 so I could get the beginning of my solo punched in. The other guys were just sitting there relaxing—they must've known how great they played. I was thinking that this was one of those trial-by-fire episodes that life gives us from time to time. The next track came along, all these guys played great (I kind of rushed the time), and then the piano player blew through another keeper right after mine. Then my voice came through the control room speakers to the engineer: "Uhhhh . . . It's me again. . . . Could we rewind and give me one more shot?" I did okay. It was time for a quick talk to my inner self.

"Don't you think that it would be better if we played up to at least our normal par today?"

"Easy for you to say! Don't you realize who's in this room with us?"

"That's my point! Why don't we get inspired from all this talent and quit with the awestruck, we-can't-play-to-save-our-life routine?"

"Well, at least we caught the solo entrance last time."

"Yeah, but rushing the time on a Nashville session? It just isn't done!"

"No argument there. I see your point. Let's go back to that basic idea that we always think about at times like this. You know which idea I'm talking about: we're doing this because we love the music. We've practiced, we've prepared, now let's just relax and crawl into the music because this is what we love to do."

"You're right. It's probably okay for a small-town guy to have the jitters for a few takes, anyway. Let's find the pocket and stay there."

This all happened in the space of a few seconds, but there was an amazing transformation. At the same time, Marcel offered a few generous words of encouragement to all, and assured me that there was no problem. The ice was definitely broken now, and I was able to feel much better about nearly every other solo. Especially helpful was the feeling that everybody was pulling together to make each track special.

An interesting thing began to happen. One of life's mysteries is how you play better some times than others. Here was a case where keeping company with some red-hot players made me play better on some takes than I would have alone. I remembered some advice that Pat Metheny gave me when we were at University of Miami School of Music: "You'll be surprised what will happen to your playing when you surround yourself with great players." I've always felt lucky to be able to play with the musicians I've been involved with on every project, and this session was a one-time burst of inspiration.

Above all was the fact that Marcel, our producer and engineer, kept the atmosphere easygoing and was comfortable putting unusual combinations of sounds together. He exhibited great leadership skills, which made for a great feeling among the whole group. His whole approach was to get a terrific session by sharing the spotlight.

One last thing. All of my favorite players share a few very important attribute; they're nice, genuine people. Marcel was always a gentleman to every person I ever saw him speak to. One of the things that I treasure about my career is the time I spend getting to work with people I admire. Thanks for an unforgettable session and warm friendship, Marcel.

How'd You Do That?

You might not even remember the first time you taught a guitar lesson. You know, when one of your friends said, "Hey man, how'd you do that?" At a very early stage in a playing career, it seems some people like to share knowledge while others want to be like magicians—they never tell the secrets. From what I've seen, most guitarists are glad to show anyone some of their favorite licks. The problem is, sometimes they can be a little difficult to teach.

If you've read this column before, you know that I have this twisted desire to try to change the way people think about making a living with music. Teaching lessons has been a reasonable way to survive for thousands of guitarists while they pursue their recording and/or performing careers. Here's a few of the things that I would like to see more teachers think about.

Instant gratification. It goes against the grain of most academic approaches, but let's face it: we are all more interested in progress that we can actually see. So make sure that after each lesson, the student can point to some actual, tangible riff, chord, song, scale, or technique. This is the teacher's insurance policy that the student will come back for more lessons, especially if that tangible evidence is a particularly musical piece of progress. Be on the lookout for music that has catchy, repetitive guitar parts. The repetitive part makes a song relatively easy to teach while the musical part makes it easier to practice. (A classic example is the guitar intro to The Doors' version of "House of the Rising Sun." The rhythm and pattern are very repetitive but musical, and they involve a series of chords, almost like a classical study.)

Develop new skills. All too often, teachers spend a whole lesson saying, "No, that finger goes there . . . Not there, over here . . . Yeah, like that, but down one fret . . . no . . . yeah . . . ." Try taking a break from that and work on some other skills, like ear training. With your advanced students you could actually work up a challenging routine where you try to guess what note each of you is playing without looking at the other's fretboard. You can really get a lot done in a few minutes when you are both firing notes back and forth at each other every few seconds. If you're dealing with a newcomer, just try to get them to recognize octave notes, or the difference between major and minor chords, or play a major scale leaving out the last note to see if they can sing it or find it on their guitar.

Be accessible as a performer. It's always helpful for a student to see the teacher demonstrate mastery of the instrument. If you're one of the people who thinks that teaching offers no incentive to those who teach, try putting yourself on a steady schedule of playing something new to your students every two weeks in a performance setting. That could mean inviting them down to the gig you play every weekend, or even getting a bunch of people to come over to your local music store after hours or to a rehearsal room. You're much more likely to light a fire under someone when they walk away saying, "I can't wait until I can play like that!"

Be observant. Or, in some cases, omniscient. Seriously, you have to realize that everyone has a different motivation, expectation, talent, and amount of time to spend practicing. Find a realistic goal for each person that fits them, and make it come true. As I'm sitting here writing this, it seems so simple to spew out all this advice. Obviously, the hard part is staying focused when you have four back-to-back lessons after a long day of other busy work. How do you do it? Well, it's simple, you just . . .

Remember the big picture. You learn, you pass it on, they help you pay your rent and bills so you can learn more. It's like the circle of life, and it works. If you can't find a good reason to really try to connect with a student who's helping to pay your bills, then you shouldn't teach. It would be better to have less teachers than to have more teachers that hate teaching. I still believe that people who are really in tune to music can see things in life that others might miss. If you are in tune to music, then you absolutely must be able to care about someone else enough to give your best.

Be creative. You could have a different approach for each student, give discount points for students who appear to practice between lessons, organize ensembles of compatible students, publish your own practice books, do a live recording at the end of each lesson strictly for fun, use a computer-based interactive system, etc. The only rule is that you've got to do your best and give something good to the people who come to you ready to learn.

Balance. If you're teaching while pursuing your own musical goals, don't let yourself get loaded down with so many students that you start to dread going to your lessons. It's much better to drive an old car and have two roommates and be an effective teacher than to have a few more bucks but resent the time you put in with your students. Luckily for everyone, there are some people who really find challenge and reward in teaching, and will want to do it full time. You might want to give it a try and see if you're one of them.

"The Number One Killer"

It seems like people are always quoting various things as being the number one cause of this or that. It has recently been brought to mind that the number one killer of bands is having the wrong attitude. So here I am, still touring all over the place, and I'm talking with lots of people at these guitar clinics that I've been doing before the shows. Everyone seems to be having three problems with their groups:

1. Personality clashes/lack of conviction
2. Wanting record deals or more live gigs
3. Needing better songs, performance, and arrangements

The only problem is, nobody mentions numbers 1 or 3. They all think that their problems would be solved by a record deal which would (they think) give them more gigs and all that good stuff. Okay, we know that it is possible for a record company to go out and sign a band based on the fact that they are exactly in the style of a competing company's latest chart topper and then proceed to ram that band down the public's throat, but . . . In the majority of cases, record companies want *everyone* to be impressed with any band that they sign. In addition, they want to make sure that most of the bands they sign can present themselves so well onstage that they virtually sell themselves to the public as they tour. Songs? You'd better have some strong ones if you expect to be considered at all. Like I said, there are no exceptions, such as an act relying heavily on some gimmick factor. Even in those cases, you'll find that even a jaded musician will admit there is usually some genuine talent behind all that.

So what makes me think that numbers 1 and 3 are the real problems with so many groups? Between talking to musicians and hearing their tapes, that's how. First, let me say that I have mixed feelings about putting relative values on supposedly artful things like songwriting, but there are some things that seem so obviously uncomfortable to listen to that I will stay with the concept that some songs could stand to be changed or improved. Songwriting weakness usually jumps right out of a tape, and performance problems that could easily be fixed are present on literally every tape I've heard recently. I'm not talking about getting a great sound or even an original sound, just playing in time and in tune. If a part is too hard to play on a demo, then find a different part, especially if you can't play your part with total conviction. It's really true that demos don't have to be perfect, but they have to show at least a crude representation of amazing talent, or a hard-fought effort to bring out the best of more typical talent. One way or another, there should be something remarkable to listen to.

On to the attitude. When I use the word "attitude," I'm not talking about the euphemism recently made popular which refers to someone sneering into the camera. I'm talking about the way that one handles and deals with things. Anytime a group breaks up, you can usually find the reason in a difference of attitude. The cliché that someone has left a band for "musical differences" is just another way of saying that there was a difference in attitude about the responsibilities, rights, and opportunities given to that band. I'm really beginning to believe that guitarists should study Dale Carnegie and the Holy Book at the same time as they study the instrument. Even solo performers will end up working with lots of others as they attempt to get agents, managers, assistants, and audience rapport.

Let's try an example of how attitude changes things. At a group's first get-together, they remain very open-minded. Everyone is saying things like, "It's fine with me either way, whatever you want to jam on." Eventually, if the group stays together, it's because some common ground was discovered that gave everyone some satisfaction. Now, fast forward a few years later when the attitude is, "We're doing my song or I'm out of here" or, "That's never going to work. We shouldn't waste time with that." This is from members of the group that got together only because everyone had the attitude to find common ground in the beginning.

Or maybe the guitarist said this to himself earlier on, "I've got to improve every day, no matter what." Fast forward to the second album where it's changed a bit–"I'll start practicing after this record company party tonight. The only reason I missed practicing the last few days is because I haven't really felt like it."

So what's it going to be? "I don't feel like playing any more crappy club gigs," or "We've got to keep playing what we all believe in no matter what!" Will you say, "I'm not going to ever speak to him again!" or "Let's talk this through. We both want the same thing in the end, right?" Have you ever thought, "I think I had a little too much to drink, maybe my playing is beginning to suffer." Or will you pull the ever-popular "I don't have a drinking problem, it's them that are causing everything to fall apart."

Statistics can be misleading, but in this case the numbers are clear. Nine out of 10 Steve Morses agree that attitude is the number 1 killer of enterprising musicians.

Learning Japanese

It turns out that Deep Purple is a very international band. This leg of our journey brings us to a relatively long Japanese tour. I'm sitting here writing this next to the window of my room, with yet another view of an endless city stretching out in all directions. What does this have to do with playing music? I absolutely promise that it will be connected to a relevant point. There's a lot to be learned from traveling here, and I wish that every American was able to visit and compare cultures more often. In case you're not planning a trip here anytime soon, let me give you some admittedly subjective impressions.

First of all, Japan is crowded—packed with people. Every square inch of space is utilized and valued. When you take psychology in high school, they tell you about the study where crowding rats together makes them more aggressive and weird . . you know, like American cities. The comparison doesn't seem to apply here, though. The people all wait for the proper traffic signals before walking across intersections, they always show basic etiquette when dealing with others, and often you'll see people with colds wearing a face mask so as not to infect others. Violent crime is incredibly low, and the only time I heard a driver honk his horn was to make a pedestrian aware that a car was carefully coming by.

In Japan, it is common for a person to remain employed by a corporation for life, not just until something better comes along. I see it in the music business people that I hang around. There is always the experienced mentor followed and assisted by the understudy or apprentice (my terms—I don't know what the Japanese call the process). You'll find that the mentor is always patient with the apprentice, and never threatens his job or talks about how easily he can be replaced. The apprentice does indeed endure some insults from time to time, but always in a joking manner so as not to weaken his loyalty.

Pride in one's work is phenomenally apparent. Every worker in a construction site is in uniform and they actually hustle to get their project moving along. Your taxi or limo driver will most likely be wearing clean white gloves and be in uniform while you sit back on perfectly white seat covers. If you buy some food to go, you'll see a very well-thought-out, careful job of packing that food before they hand it to you.

So how does this relate to, say, playing in a band? Well, grab a few of these ideas and imagine what benefit could come of them, like consideration for others, loyalty in jobs, patience for extended preparation of job skills, pride of workmanship, and on and on. Let's take an example.

Imagine your group at rehearsal. Everybody is getting restless because Jim is late again, and some of the guys haven't taken the trouble to learn the song that was supposed to be quickly tried before starting on the original material. Two guys are already getting trashed on whatever, and everybody's complaining that the business sucks.

What could be different using some Japanese ways? First, another disclaimer—Yes, I know that the Japanese have some built-in sociological advantages and that they are not the only people on the planet that embrace the ideas that I mentioned earlier. And I know that a one-page column can't always be perfectly politically correct and . . . anyway, start with Jim being late. The same peer pressure that the Japanese exert on themselves to do right can work with Jim. But the reason it seems to work in Japan is that so many are actually following the rule in question. In other words, what if everybody made it a point to really start on time, even if someone was late? Jim might feel a little more urgency to get there on time if he knew that the rest of the band was starting at noon no matter what, as opposed to thinking, "Ah, everybody's late for Saturday practice all the time, no big deal."

So when Jim arrives, instead of threatening to replace him, see him as a person that could use some assistance with time management; offer to pick him up next time, for example. In other words, you be the mentor since you've figured out how to arrive on time and he hasn't. Don't belittle him for it; see it as something that you will patiently work on together. Same with the guys who didn't do their homework assignment of learning that cover tune. If most of the people in the group are on the ball, it will tend to make the others sink or swim. As far as the guys who are useless because they're getting wasted, send them home but give them a role model in yourself—and another chance. You can't change things like that overnight, and sadly, sometimes not at all.

Things are really different in the States. Don't let that stop you from using your brain to learn from others. We've brought all kinds of different cultural influences to one place and mixed them up, and that's cool, but let's separate the good from the bad as often as possible. By the way, stimulating your mind to do your music better can be very beneficial to your country. It seems that entertainment (recordings, movies, software) is one of the few things that help lessen our trade deficit.

New Motivation

Do you make New Year's resolutions and that kind of stuff? I do, sort of. It's a good time to think about what was good about the past year and what could stand some improvement. Since I've spent most of the last year seeing the world with Deep Purple, my perspective is definitely going to be different now. So I'll tell you some of the things that stick out as great foundations for new motivation. I'll put them in the categories of "things to improve" and "things that were cool."

Things To Improve

Practicing habits. While I generally can find enough time in noisy environments to do some technical warm up and things that don't require too much concentration, I have found that my only truly quiet time is late after the gig in my hotel room. I should find a way to more often set aside some quiet time during the day to be with my guitar. My theory is that two small but effective sessions a day are often more productive than one longer single session. Sometimes when I'm having a problem getting ready to start a run of dates, I find that practicing twice a day provides more benefit than the number of minutes spent would suggest.

A more balanced diet. I definitely ate too much pizza in so many countries. But, on the other hand, it was the only thing available in many places that I could recognize.

I should be more amazed at life itself instead of having to experience a nearly perfect gig to feel uplifted on the road. Many people within the group had friends or family fall ill or even die during the course of the year. Since it eventually happens to everyone, I guess all of us get somewhat dulled to the fact that just being alive is miraculous. That's what big numbers will do for you—there are billions of people, so we simply accept that overwhelming fact; same with records or blockbuster movies. If they become so well-known, then people dismiss them as common and they're unable to appreciate them as much.

Sleep. I really must figure out how to get sleep like a normal person. Changing time zones as easily as tempos from song to song just flips out my internal clock. On the other hand, I should look at the positive side of being a very light sleeper—I could be a great guard dog.

Phone bills. It's not surprising that calls from Slovenia or Poland are expensive, but I continue to regard phone bills as documents that just don't look right without being deep in the four figure range. In Europe, many of the other guys are set with little digital phones that seem to work with no problem from one country to another, but they're not yet compatible with our U.S.-type phones.

I must remember what a reasonably priced nation the U.S. is. Everywhere else you go constantly reminds me of that fact. I will try hard to remember that this year as I quickly adjust back to normal outrage at the prices of things today. Amazingly, the things that are available in the U.S. that come from abroad are almost always less expensive here.

Our social interaction. Many other countries seem to have safe streets and community events with no fear of walking or riding bikes in any part of their cities. It's up to us to say enough is enough. Writing a sentence about it won't change much, but what if everyone just suddenly knew that it didn't have to keep on getting worse? Someone once told me that we get what we settle for. Hmmm…

Things That Were Cool

Getting to talk to my five-year-old son every day at an age where he can entertain me on the phone with his unique views on the way things are. My favorite time was when he asked me to hold on while he got something to eat. I thought he was just going to grab something and come right back to the phone. But since I was paying the Moscow rate of eight dollars a minute from the hotel because of some problem with my carrier, of course he just forgot to return to the phone. After holding for ten minutes then trying back until they hung up the phone, he then requested that I make up another story to tell him. Well, I never will get tired of doing that.

I have been surrounded by great, supportive people in the group. I will never again underestimate the importance of good chemistry between people. Two nights ago I had a terribly frustrating technical problem all through the show and I was not handling it very well, especially at first. Everyone was surprisingly helpful in getting me past the point that was ruining the show for me. Instead of getting upset at me for showing some frustration, Ian came over and said that he's really glad that I have that much passion for what I am doing. That made all the difference in the world. One minute life sucks, the next I'm feeling thankful. Everyone knew exactly what I was going through and naturally chose to help up one of their wounded. That's good chemistry, and I still don't know if it's luck or destiny or effort that makes it happen, but I'm glad it does. There are also plenty of stories like that from every group I've worked with. When I was a kid wanting to start a band, that was the main reason I was drawn to it. You know, the sum is greater than the parts.

Foreign exchange. If you ever went to a club gig of the Dregs or my band, you could almost always talk to me afterwards. It's kind of normal to be somewhat accessible when you're playing clubs, especially if you're in a band that's doing multiple sets. I got into the habit of greeting those that were able to stick around after the show, because of a guitarist who spent some time talking to me when I was a kid at one of my first shows. In the process of this last year, I've met and learned about a lot of people from many places, backgrounds, and professions. Some of it has been the most valuable education in my whole life.

Goodwill. I've met busloads of Croatians traveling a long way to see the show, and other hard working people in nearly every country who travel great distances to be a part of it. People everywhere have brought gifts, good wishes, enthusiasm, and energy to those large places that our fearless crew has seen everyday at set up time. I've seen opening bands bust their butts to get on and off stage on time after driving all night. People planning their vacations around the tour because they love the energy of live music. Yeah, again and again, I always have to agree that music can strike pretty deep.

Into the Comfort Zone

I just got back from doing a few gigs with my trio, and it was a great experience. I was wondering if I could even remember the material at first, but by the end I felt confident playing it. The transformation wasn't instantaneous, of course, but it went at a steady, progressive pace. In fact, that's a good reason to take on projects that seem a little beyond your comfort zone—you can see a change in a relatively short amount of time.

The reason that playing a few gigs with Dave [LaRue, bassist] and Van [Romaine, drummer] was initially beyond the comfort zone was that we hadn't played any gigs together for about a year. The entire year I was on trips with Deep Purple, and these trio gigs were scheduled for the day after Christmas, which nixed any plans of band rehearsal since Van was out of town. The first order of business was to put together a new set list. Dave has a natural talent for organization as well as music, so he compiled the list. We wanted to change the show around from the last time we were out, despite the fact that our only rehearsals would be at soundchecks. Luckily, we all had recordings of the new songs we wanted to play, so it was just a matter of lots of homework to learn and review the material.

Figuring out how to reduce an arrangement for a live trio usually involves deciding which elements of an existing arrangement (in this case, the one from the album) would be missed. I found that sometimes it helps to totally change the bass line when I'm making a transition from a chord-heavy section to a single-line part. When I'm playing a melody up high, it leaves a lot of room for Dave to put in more movement or even polyphony in the bass. Often in a recording I'll repeat a theme several times, with different overdubs being added each time to build the song. But during a live version, we usually cut down the number of repetitions so it doesn't become stagnant without those overdubs. Fadeouts on the recordings also present a problem for live shows, so we have to come up with endings that everyone can remember easily. The best way seems to be using some theme or riff from the tune in the ending.

One tune had a long improvised section on the original recording, and our challenge was to get in and out of the section while keeping it improvisational and free. The solution was to use a small musical cue from the recorded version that would signal the other guys that a change was coming up. This is my standard way to get out of any solo section that doesn't have a specified number of bars.

In this case, one of the musical cues that I chose felt perfectly natural to me, but it threw Dave off since he was hearing it as the middle of a phrase whereas I heard it as a beginning. After checking the recording we were not surprised to find Dave was correct. I was allowing a two-bar pause near the beginning of the solo, then referencing everything from that point. Anyway, it was no big deal to straighten out.

Memorizing material that I'd played only a few times, and a long time ago, brought out some mnemonic tricks that might come in handy for you as well. Simply reviewing the entire arrangement, even to yourself, is a good way to get the big picture into focus. I also always visualize difficult parts. The concept of visualization is to actually see, in your mind's eye, the fingering of each note and hear the sound in your head as well. It's an excellent memory tool as long as you go slowly enough to get every note perfectly programmed in your mind. Visualization is a way to explore different fingerings for difficult passages. Even while I'm driving, I'll go over sections in my mind on different parts of the neck to see where it seems more comfortable. Sounds odd, but there's no doubt that practicing in your mind helps. Of course, there are some things that you just can't do without a guitar in your hands, like working on your technique.

Just think of it like training for a marathon. You can't do all your training in the first day, although most of us try to. When I play a tune like "Stressfest," it's going to be a waste of time if my chops aren't up, so I have to get in shape fast. Luckily, it had only been a few short weeks since the Deep Purple tour ended, so when the trio played I really just had to concentrate on specific things that had slipped a little during the brief time off, like playing very fast 16ths. Playing the passages smoothly and calmly proved to be harder than I thought, so I used another practice method the last four days before the gig. The method involved practicing at least twice a day, even if the sessions were short. For some reason, breaking up my practicing like this gives me more rapid improvement with finite, measurable things such as technique. When I need to get over a picking problem, I slow down and find which movements are more difficult. In most cases I can get instant improvement by working on only, say, upstrokes for few minutes. As I've said many times before, to improve your technique quickly, concentrate on the weak spots. Weak spots can be brought down to a note-by-note level which will show what the technical flaw is. Just work on the flaws and then play it again slowly to see what pops out as a problem. This is much better than just repeating the same thing over and over *with* mistakes at performance tempo. Remember that you can perform differently than you practice.

So, back to what I was saying in the beginning: Planning musical events just slightly outside of your comfort zone will yield tremendous results. Realistically, there is no way that I would have come up with as stimulating a practice challenge if it had not been for the fact that we had to scramble to get ready for these gigs. Moral of the story? Jump back in and schedule yourself some more performance time—but be sure to add some new material or some new element of challenge. Good luck. Now I've got to go work on my banjo vibrato.

Driven to Succeed

Don't hide it. I've done it, you've done it. . . . When time is tight, you're hungry, and you live in America, there's a good chance that a well-placed drive-through window will get your business sooner or later. The interesting thing about it is that the lines at the drive-through can be longer than the ones inside, but many people still won't get out of their cars and walk in. Too much trouble, right? So, you've got people spending more time waiting for the convenience of fast food, which has limited choices *because* it's fast.

Now, what would happen if people approached their guitars with the same intensity that they go for the drive-through? Everyone would be pretty familiar with their instruments. "I'll try a V chord, hold the major 3rds, and make the solo broiled—hot, not cold and mushy like it was last time." We would make excuses for the fact that it seems a lot easier at first to play electronic synths with computerized composing software. What is the big appeal of the drive-through and how does this guitar metaphor relate?

Well, for one thing, hunger is one of the main motivators of all humans. It's absolutely primal. And if you have ever felt completely exhilarated by music, or unleashed the primal beast within you during a heavy solo, then you have a clue. Make the experience of playing the guitar always feed some of that basic hunger that attracts you to music in the first place. How? Always give a little practice time to your favorite things to play after you've made some accomplishments or discoveries during your normal practice. Another way might be to do most of your practice session without an amp, then at the end, after you're really warmed up, plug in and treat your ears to the result of all that hard work.

Along the same lines, having a recent show to think about or an upcoming show to prepare for can keep the rush of live playing in the front of your mind and help motivate you. Best of all, though, has got to be simply having a burning desire to get on your guitar every day and see what can happen. This is one of the main reasons that I always consider desire to be more important than almost anything else for someone starting out in music. Think about what made you start to play in the first place. Try to stay in touch with that feeling when you remember what it was.

Of course, sometimes the passion and desire to play can run a bit low. I went through this conversation in my head just the other day. Sometimes you're just beat from a long day, or in the wrong mood, and just don't feel like making your way over to the corner and opening up the guitar case. I find, in those times, that if I just push myself to commit to the first five minutes, I'm usually drawn right in. Before I know it, I'm having a great time and coming up with something that refuels the desire.

During those five minutes, try something different. Just close your eyes and jam on something simple, or try changing the parameters by playing in different rhythmic groupings, modes, or playing the melody of the last thing you heard on the radio. Or try picking out the harmonies of that soundtrack to the TV show you just turned off. I bet you'll find that once the guitar is in your hands, you will want to spend a little time with it—and the more reasons you give yourself to practice, the more time you'll spend each day.

We're often drawn to our instrument because we love the guitar's sound, we feel pride in accomplishing something on it, and we want to excel. In application, that means giving yourself a better chance to make it through a public performance. I'm not sure why, but most people will appear more neat and their homes will look a bit more organized when they know that guests are coming over; the same thing works for practicing. If company is coming over soon—like when you're going to be in front of a bunch of people who will notice if you do well or not at the gig next weekend—you're more likely to get things in order. While you're cleaning up your act, try not to sweep all the problems under the rug.

On with the Show

As we came to the end of our second song, I watched the entire PA and lighting tower buckle down and fall into the crowd as if in slow motion. There were at least 60 guys who had climbed up to get a better view, and now they were leaping into the rows of innocent people below to break their fall. Within a few seconds, there was a huge jet of sparks as the high-voltage power lines near the collapsing framework were cut and shorted. I held my breath waiting to see if our light and sound guys would make it out of there without being burned or electrocuted. By the light of the melting and arcing copper wiring, I saw only one of them get out for sure.

This was a jammed Deep Purple stadium show in the country of Chile, and we were told that it is just a sign of excitement when people throw various items onstage like shirts, hats, banners, other unidentified and perhaps previously worn garments, and coins. At this point the lights were out everywhere and vocalist Ian Gillan was saying over the microphone that everybody should stay still and be quiet. But the main sound system was out and all that was working was the monitor system. In the darkness and confusion, the pieces of gear and rigging being thrown around couldn't be identified. We were ushered back to the dressing room.

Once we all got to the door, someone said aloud what we were all thinking: "I sure hope nobody was killed." Originally it looked as if this was to be one of those great shows where more people showed up than anyone had anticipated. But before the show even started, a number of people had started climbing over the walls, presumably without tickets. It was kind of a crazy mob scene, and a riot was a very real possibility now that we had stopped the show after only about seven minutes. If they could tear down a fence, and then destroy a large metal structure, they might get angry about having spent money on a show that looked like it was over just as it started.

We were told to leave until facts were gathered about injuries and the possibilities of hooking up some kind of sound-mixing capability. The band was not too excited about leaving, and we decided that waiting around wouldn't be too bad of an idea. After seeing the sound and light boards smashed and covered with twisted metal, we were relieved to see that our guys Alan and Pat were okay, though Pat was looking bloody from a cut. Finally, we relaxed when we heard that nobody was killed or critically injured and the crowd was staying in control. Maybe we could still revive the show.

The stadium was still full. The sound and light boards were dead, so we ran the PA off the monitor mix, wired a bank of lights, and went back on.

The place went completely bonkers with this kind of violent mosh pit in full force near the front of the stage. There was so much pent-up energy and angst from this disaster that some of these guys were getting too weird. Security was spending all their time throwing water at these people being trapped and crushed at the front of the stage. Any females or couples had long since abandoned this war zone in front of us. As I bent down to beg a security man to stop this brain-dead guy from spitting at the band, he asked me for a guitar pick and did nothing else. By the way, if you are like me, having someone spit at you is a huge insult, right? Apparently in Chile it is expected, somewhat tolerated, and even somehow construed as a twisted, aggressive form of approval. This is the explanation that dozens of people gave me after the show. I'm not making this up!

Anyway, imagine playing a solo with your eyes closed and suddenly your face is splattered with someone else's spit. Nice mental picture, eh? My eyes popped open and I motioned to the group in front of me to point to who did it. They just smiled and asked for picks. Ian, who had been in the exact same situation years before, walked over and wiped my face with a towel without missing a beat. Now, I, the spittee, had unwittingly given the spitter my approval to continue his target practice by showing my animated reaction. After all, if every rock band looked angry for every publicity shot, then these kinds of fans must really be in heaven when they acted angry, too, right? I'm really not making this up.

By now we'd had the equivalent of a major garage sale worth of clothing thrown up onstage, the security staff in front of us thought that their only job was to grab guitar picks, the lights that had been hard-wired on full brightness were smelling kind of funny, Robert the monitor man was so busy that changing the monitor mix seemed like an inappropriate request, and Ian was starting to slide around on the saliva-soaked stage. I began a mantra in my head: "I'm a professional, I'm going to finish this gig. . . ." I found myself wondering what the penalty was for murder in between each positive thought. The spit snipers fired literally every time I momentarily got back into the music and closed my eyes, but still I wouldn't move back to the safe no-fire zone. Luckily, there were no more hits above the neck; in fact, very few hits at this point. It was safe to say that this wasn't what my parents had in mind when they saved each hard-earned penny toward my education, but it turned out that even this day was a big learning experience.

At the end of the last encore, there was a breakthrough in the case: I, the spittee, made brief eye contact with the spitter. He gave the unmistakable gesture that he was proud of his work and would like to make more meaningful contact. As the smoke poured from each of my ears, I pictured an airline cockpit checklist: *Logic? "Off." Reasoning ability? "Bypassed." Adrenaline? "High pressure boost position." Tunnel vision? "100 percent." Brain temperature? "150 percent overload! Abort! Abort!"*

I heard my guitar hit the stage after the last note and suddenly I was down in the pit heading for my new friend. As my left hand was in motion and just a few inches away from showing my appreciation, the comatose security guys suddenly found something to do. With both of my arms immobilized, someone, presumably my new friend, had a hold of my neck in an unfriendly way. Someone stole a precious momento from our African trip that I was wearing on a necklace. Then I was traveling backwards, writhing in an attempt to break loose, but most definitely traveling backwards and up toward the stage. The crowd had been roaring the whole time as the band took their bows. They roared a bit more for me, the guy who looked like he was going into the crowd to shake hands and give away picks. The first wave of a huge sea of embarrassment hit me as I realized tens of thousands of people had a great time—heck, the spitters probably did, too. I actually finished the gig, though, and except for a few guys in front, the crowd thought I was warmly thanking them by jumping down. I felt like a real politician (getting credit for something unintended), but I made no more embarrassing moves and headed offstage to drench my face with disinfectant.

They told me that the main spitter got chased out of the stadium by the guys in front. Soon after, we played one of the best shows ever in another packed venue, and this time there were absolutely no problems or conflicts. Life on the road is as good as I can imagine. This will help me keep in mind why I'm out here as I review all the things I will do differently, or just not do next time there's a little weirdness.

This month's "Open Ears" is dedicated to those innocent people who got knocked down. I hope you get a laugh from reading about my slapstick adventure onstage, and thank God there were no serious injuries to any of you.

A New Worldview

Lately I've noticed a definite correlation between where I tour and what I write about in this column. In short, I think that the best aspects of travel are being exposed to new cultures and discovering different ways of thinking, doing, or learning. As a result, I've got plenty to think and write about now, just three days after visiting much of South America.

For instance, I noticed how differently people react to being famous in their own country. One day I was being interviewed at a hotel in Brazil by three guys from a magazine. One of them was asking me some technical questions. Based on the types of questions he asked, I could tell he was a guitarist, but he never went into any detail about himself. We had a time limitation, and everyone stayed focused on getting the job done. Everybody was very nice, and we all said good-bye and I went on to a gig or something.

Several days later I learned that he was playing guitar in one of the big MTV bands of Brazil and was very good. He had just come along to ask some questions for his friends at the magazine. Now imagine any guitarist from a successful U.S. band doing this and not even asking "Don't you know who I am?" He understood that the job at hand was more important than a power trip. I'm not bringing this up to say that we don't know how to do things here in the U.S.; I just want to show some different attitudes that I saw in my travels.

A few days later, I was doing a guitar seminar at a music conservatory and I recognized my Portuguese/English language interpreter as a guitarist featured in the latest guitar magazine. No big deal. He just wanted to help translate some of the peculiar guitar terms to the native tongue—another great guy who had no problem with the real world. One of our shows had an opening band from Brazil that was quite well known, and they also turned out to be pretty nice. A guy working at a radio station was a musician in yet another band that had received some widespread press. He had no problem with the fact that he still had a day job; he just had to work a little harder to keep the band going.

I know there are stories similar to these in the States, but it's definitely a question of degree. Is it possible that you'll find instances like these on occasion? Sure. Is it likely that you'll always find instances like these? Not really.

The story doesn't end there. Three men traveled a long distance and waited a long time to show us some of their guitars. Now, this happens all the time, no matter what, so I braced myself for the hard-sell spiel about why I should buy one of their instruments. I couldn't blame them for trying to make a living, so I tried to concentrate on what they were saying. In actuality, they wanted to get some honest suggestions and criticism on their work in order to improve it. Like I said, you can find these kinds of stories almost anywhere, but I'm still impressed and amazed every single time I see people who really give it their all.

It's easy for us to lose perspective on things. (Ask me how I know.) For example, think about how many opportunities we have to acquire knowledge and equipment and to network with other musicians here. Now try to imagine a place where the nearest music store has just three guitars, no music lessons, and is a hellish 19-hour bus ride away. Imagine that ordering music on CD is all you can afford from the fruits of your day job. I couldn't imagine it, yet I talked to some musicians who spent their life savings and days of travel to come to the high mountains of Bolivia, where we did an outdoor gig. They learned English by trading imported Guitar magazines and reading album credits and lyrics.

Shifting gears slightly, I guess the real lesson I learned is that we don't have any shortage of talent in the United States; motivation seems to be the only thing that everyone needs help with. Maybe that's why I always tell people to play what they love if they want to do it for a living. It's just easier to stay motivated when you're working on something you really care about. In truth, the people I met on my travels would probably change a little bit if they were put in our environment for some time. But in the long run, I think that if you really want to play the guitar, you'll be motivated to do so.

So what do you do to stay motivated? How about doing something every single day to move yourself closer to your goal? That might include working on sight reading, transcribing something that seemed too difficult yesterday, working out different fingerings for a melody you already know, writing better music, recording demos, and so on. By keeping that rule and accomplishing something every day, you'll actually build yourself up in more ways than one. First, you'll be more motivated every time you accomplish a task that once seemed too big. Second, you'll be more confident as you begin to see all big tasks as just a series of small ones. Third, and best of all, you'll actually make progress toward mastering your instrument.

What about the days that you feel too tired or lazy to do anything? Keep the idea simple. If you feel bad because you're sick, listen to some music and analyze the chord structure. Think about the lyrics. Think about what you'd do differently. If you have to work the whole day, use half your lunch break to pick up your instrument and play with it. You don't have to wait until the perfect opportunity comes along to spend time improving your skills. Musicians who are successful in the long run just can't get enough of it. That's why I say you should play what you love, so that you'll always want more.

Contract? What Contract?

This month, I'd like to review some of the basic business ideas that can change the course of your career. It sounds like a boring topic, but if you want to make a living doing music, you have to know this: The way you think about your commitments will determine whether you're someone who thinks "the world owes me" and for whom nothing ever seems to happen, or someone for whom things are constantly getting better. How could this be such a huge deal? After all, everyone knows that playing great is all it takes, right?

Wrong. I don't want to trivialize the playing part of your career; after all, that's the part that feeds your soul and makes the difference between working in drudgery or communicating the feelings of life while making a living at the same time. But it's how you approach your commitments that will make the difference between music simply feeding your soul and also paying the bills. A key point here is that musicians have to be open-minded about dealing with structured things if they want to remain creative.

For example, if you're trying out a song idea, you'll get far if you have some fun with the structure and say, "Let's see how this sounds in a different tempo, or a different key, or with a different chorus. If that doesn't work, I can already see some ways to change the verse chords. . . ." Compare that attitude with, "I get up at 6:15 to catch the 7:25 train to the office. At 5:01 I leave to catch the 5:20 back home." Obviously, the very nature of writing music works well for a person who can see lots of possibilities and quickly adapt to fit them. By contrast, the people who write most of our contracts tend to follow a certain routine and use the memory feature of their word processors to "write" your contract. This isn't a slam against them, just an observation in general terms. As humans, we all have our different talents.

On the other hand, people who are business-oriented will probably have a much clearer idea of what happens to someone at work who can't fulfill their commitments or who is always blowing off appointments. Harsh realities like this don't occur so much in the musician's mind, because typically they're focused on the music more than the realities of the music business. So, to briefly revisit my original point, I think this is one of the reasons that otherwise intelligent musicians end their careers with mistakes that most people in the general work force would be able to recognize.

By the way, I'm writing about this because I keep seeing promising musicians living in total denial of the basic laws of business—or the basic rules of common sense. Why would someone skip rehearsal, be late onstage for no reason, forget promises or debts, and then complain that they can't find a gig worthy of their talent? In a case like that, the musicians themselves would fire a person who was constantly undependable. Now, what if a musician tried some stuff like that with a record company? You better believe that their record sales would have to be fantastic to keep them from getting the boot. To take it one step further, most record companies have a "Business Affairs" department that will yank your contract out of the file at any vice president's request and find one of a dozen ways to legally ream you. Rather than say you should outsmart them with the best, most sneakily worded contract and expect them to sign it, I'll suggest the most radical concept to deal with anyone: Say what you mean and mean what you say.

If you said you'd do something, then just plain do it, to the best of your ability. If you signed a document that says that you'll do something, then pretend that your signature is worth something and that your word is too. If you prove to any company that you can be counted on to produce what you promise, then those 80 pages of contract that give them every possible way to sue, punish, garnish, seek indemnification, or otherwise belittle you will never get pulled out of the filing cabinet. Sure, they'll always have the ammunition, but that's the price of being the seller in a buyer's market. In this instance of a record contract, you can only change the degree of imbalance slightly by having a team of attorneys working for you to negotiate what the company is willing to put on paper. Companies that are flooded with prospective acts looking for any shot at all are not going to be putting a lot of concessions on paper. I say, get what you reasonably can, then forget about it and get to work.

As far as gigs go, the contracts at the level where many of us work at, are frequently signed after the gig is over, or not at all. From my viewpoint, I can't remember the last time that I signed a fully executed contract for a gig. I'm sure I have, but it's been awhile. In this case, it's all about credibility. Let's look at an example.

Joe's showcase nightclub has an opening three weeks away that you'd like to fill. If he's going to have a chance to sell tickets, he's going to have to print the tickets and put them on sale the moment that your agent confirms over the phone. By the time the contracts are done, he's already printed tickets and hired sound and lights for the night. How do you think Joe will react when a band with a reputation for sometimes not showing up asks for a date just a few weeks away? Of course, Joe will want the paperwork to be all done before he even orders the tickets, so the date will never happen on such short notice, or maybe at all.

The downside of working things out over the phone is that misunderstandings can occur. Say the agent talks up a date to a club and the club is ready to go for it. The agent says, "I'll get back to you on that." Then the agent calls up the act's manager and says, "Look at this offer and let me know if you want to do it." The manager says, "I'll have to call you on Monday. The road manager needs to see if they can manage that distance from where they'll be the night before." Meanwhile, the club pencils in the date because the agent sounded so positive that it would be approved, and someone at the club sees it written in and puts an ad in the paper. After the road manager explains to the manager that there's no way to travel 950 miles in eight hours in a truck, the agent eventually calls the club to let them know that it's not possible. Next thing that you know, the ad in the paper has "CANCELED" in big letters over the night that has your act's name. You never even knew about the gig and lots of people in that town are wondering why "you canceled," Obviously, there's nothing you can do in this case, and yes, it does happen with some regularity.

But let's concentrate on the things that you can do something about. The spoken word is still legal to use and should be the strongest contract you ever make. Your end of the bargain—just keep it.

Mind Over Gig

Just as mind works over matter, how you mentally prepare for a gig can make all the difference in your performance. Head trips and mind games can wreak havoc on your confidence, but don't think there will always be some kind of mental drama to deal with if you're a gigging guitarist. Most musicians develop a sense of humor to downplay the stressful parts of performing. While this works, it's also worth noting that playing music you love will make performing worth the stress.

This month I want to look at some practical ways to help you build your confidence for gigging. Used together, they can help to ease the stress and strain of performing as well as improve your ability to deliver the goods under pressure.

Practice Makes . . . Well, You Know
The one way to prepare your mind for any gig is to just do your homework. After you play your first time in front of people, you'll quickly learn that it's much easier to seem awesome in your home than it is to *be* awesome before an audience. Actually, that's not a bad thing, because it forces you to commit to the music. You know how phony it sounds when someone on TV reads from a teleprompter, and you know how genuine emotion can be revealed when an actor becomes the character they intended to portray. It's the same way with performing: You have to commit to sell the goods. If you know the songs cold and have your technique up and smoking, then you can relax and find the emotion that made you want to perform in the first place.

I start my mental adjustment when I'm getting ready for any gig. I remind myself that I don't want to be onstage during that first gig struggling with some technique or trying to remember the song form. At the very least, doing your homework gives some protection from panicking or feeling like you're blowing it. So, step one: Review the songs and do some improvising and technical exercises every day without fail for at least 10 days before the first gig. On the road, I find it's better for me physically if I play between shows; but more importantly, it gives me the confidence to close my eyes during a solo and just let it happen.

Get Into Your Head
Some of this mental preparation can be done while you're traveling, even if you're center seat, coach class. I'm talking about visualiza-

tion—where you see yourself with your mind's eye, correctly performing every step involved. Wherever you are, you can mentally review a list of songs and remind yourself where to change to your other pickup or switch channels; or you can go over the form of a tricky arrangement and visualize yourself looking at the other musicians when they have a solo to help you remember the form. Each time you review something in your mind and associate it with another thing, you will make it more indelible in your memory. I strongly believe in the value of visualization, so don't think that you need a practice studio to help prepare for a gig.

Positivity Equals Power
Sometimes there isn't time to prepare your mind when you really need to. Deep Purple was once booked for a show in the former Soviet Union. After arriving, I learned that most of the crew, including the only guy who knew how to hook up my rig, was not going to make the show in time. Next thing I knew, I was onstage in a T-shirt and flight jacket looking for my wires, which had been scattered across 100 feet of stage mixed with sound and light gear. There was no 110-volt power, many items of my rig seemed to be missing, nobody spoke English, and it started snowing. By the way, this is one of the stories I think of anytime someone naively says how much of a party it must be to be a musician.

There I was, on my hands and knees, trying to get enough light to figure out where the unmarked borrowed cables should go, when this guy standing in front of the stage yells in broken English, "Steven? That is you? Why you not play? Why you set up equipment now?" After enlisting a translator, I finally got power and performed a line check for monitors. We were on in ten minutes. I couldn't feel my fingers because I'd been out on this windswept, snow-flurried stage, setting up, dressed for Florida. Any thoughts of being comfortable with my instrument would have to wait until the second hour of the show. On top of it all, 12 movie cameras were recording every second of the setup and the show. Pressure, anyone?

Instead of letting it get to me, I just made up my mind that it was going to be all right. I rushed to the dressing room, wore a heavy jacket for a few minutes, put my hands around the coffee pot until I got some feeling in my fingers, and asked for a steady supply of hot water to be put on my amp case. And away we went. I can say that I went onstage with as much energy as any other night.

Your Audience Likes You. Honest.
The only way to mentally prepare for disasters and unknown changes is to truly believe that your effort is being taken into account

by the audience. If you've ever played an entire song with a broken string on a floating-bridge ax, then you know the meaning of the word *humility*. Just the fact that you tried to do it will matter. Remember the news clips of the marathon runner collapsing just before the finish? That massive effort to pick oneself up and get back in the race is what people remember most. So for unknown events, you just have to check one thing: Is your heart in this? If so, then the biggest part is covered. All aspects of being mentally prepared and confident will be easier with time.

When all is said and done, probably the best advice is to remember that this is fun. People who have to speak before a crowd are often advised to imagine their audience dressed only in their underwear. Instead, try imagining that those people are just like you—that they drove all the way to your gig and found a parking space and took out good money to buy tickets to the show because they like live music and because they want to have a good time. If you honestly want to give them their money's worth, then you've got nothing to worry about anymore. You'll all have a good time.

Ultimately, you'll just have to get out and find the routines that work for you. Play what you love—in front of people, and in various musical situations. Above all, don't forget why you love it in the first place.

Ride to Glory

You know the old saying: "Get back on the horse that threw you." It means that if you have a momentary lapse that allows the horse to get the upper hand, you have to jump right back on and establish the pecking order. This is not just for the horse's benefit but to give you confidence that you are, to some extent, in control of the equestrian beast.

Naturally (and inevitably), this fits into the world of music. Let's say you're playing a gig and you really blow it on some little section of your solo because you tried something new and it didn't work. Suddenly you're freaked out, disgusted with yourself, and not enjoying the rest of the tune. Worst of all, you allow yourself to become slightly more conservative about taking musical chances in the next tune. Does this sound like such a dire situation that we need to discuss it in this magazine? No, this little moment of making a mistake is no big deal, but the effect it has on your future direction is something to be concerned with, as we shall see in a moment.

I'm going to interrupt my example here with another analogy. Let's say you're driving a car down the boulevard and it goes to the right about one foot. You're still within the lane, so there's no problem, right? Well, that depends on whether you let the trend continue. If you keep drifting right, you'll eventually be stopped—suddenly—by a telephone pole. But if you make a correction and set the vehicle straight again, we'll all rest a little easier.

In this same way, one little minor solo section is now threatening to destroy your confidence in your improvisation. My advice? Don't let it happen. The next solo that comes up, I want you to try again to do something different than usual. It doesn't have to be spectacular, but show yourself that you can do it. The idea is to overturn that setback and get back into the music with a little accomplishment or victory, not just in this example but every time something bad happens to you.

Any time you try something that doesn't work out as well as you planned it, you will have those people who will say, "I guess you finally learned your lesson. Bet you don't try that again." The only time that type of response fits is when it refers to things that are done for negative reasons or hurt other people. If you try something musically for the purpose of making it more interesting or exciting, and it's done for a positive reason, the only response to a momentary failure is this: "I guess you didn't learn your lesson. Get back and try it again, maybe make it a little simpler." So if you make a mistake trying to harmonize spontaneously by playing your usual part up a diatonic third, then try to harmonize several other upcoming parts with the same treatment to show yourself that you can do it. Keep the same idea, but take smaller bites by trying it on shorter or simpler phrases.

But why is this so important, you're wondering? It's simple: In reality, a creative musician has to deal with the real world while cultivating the ability to compare make-believe scenarios. This means imagining what a song would sound like with one idea versus another idea and being able to structure the results into a usable form. It takes childlike imagination, knowledge, experience, and confidence—confidence that your experiments will generally be okay, or better than okay, confidence that you can attempt the unknown.

Another example relates to playing with a group. You've had a bad experience with the singer in your band, and now you're both mad at each other. So here you are, a day later, about to start a gig. Most people avoid each other once they've had words and usually expect the other person to apologize if there's going to be any peace. Apparently it's a widely held secret that the person who starts the ball rolling toward reconciliation is the strong one. That's right, and that's why you should stand up and say, "Hey man, I don't know why we got so upset with each other last night. Sorry, let's put it behind us." Not that it needs to be a contest over who's stronger, but sometimes people actually think they're protecting their "pride" by not saying "I'm sorry." In reality, they may be allowing an important relationship to decay. To me, pride would be something that comes from taking positive action as opposed to deliberately not doing anything. In my mind, when I have a little falling out with someone, I compare it to falling off that horse. I say "get back on" enough times to prove that I can ride, or that the horse is lame. I think the most creative minds we've ever known were some of the last to say "I'm beating a dead horse. I give up."

Personally, I love stories about people who never give up. I have a good friend who went up the big career roller coaster and back down. Most people would resign themselves to a life of substance abuse, alcoholism, or depression, or all of the above. This guy just kept on trying everything that he knew and got through some personal hard times. Today he's doing quite well in the business again. In fact, I know of quite a few similar stories.

The reason that this sounds like a pep talk is because it is. Did you know that Olympic athletes are placed mostly by the amount of determination that they possess? The ones that can drive themselves hard during training, even when there's no coach around, are the ones that rise above. Obviously, there's an essential ingredient of talent, but the way they approach a challenge is the key to their future. Every outstanding musician that I've been privileged to know has been characterized by talent and a nearly indestructible spirit. Feed that spirit with the little victories that will constantly come your way by jumping back on and trying again.

The Composer Within

This is not the easiest thing to write about. It's not the easiest thing to teach a person, either. But it's probably one of the things that makes or breaks most artist's careers. I'm talking about stage clothes, of course.

Actually, I'm talking about writing music—"composing," as I prefer to think of it. Ask any talent scout or A&R person what they want in a new artist, and they'll eventually say "writing ability." After stage clothes, maybe.

Writing music is part left brain, part right brain: that is, part creative, part practical. Given an unlimited amount of time, I would give greater emphasis to the creative part of composing. However, since we very seldom have the world come to a standstill until we finish a project, we need some strategies to make the most of what we come up with creatively.

First, let me repeat some of my theory of creativity. In my opinion, we are born with it. Once we are in the company of other humans, there exists a very organized system to stamp that creativity into submission. This is done to make us easier to deal with in school and at home, and it basically revolves around following rules. These rules usually begin with the word "don't." I'm not an anarchist, I'm just telling it like I see it. I mean, I don't want a world full of out-of-control maniacs either, okay?

Nevertheless, the emphasis is on conforming to a previously conceived way to be. Parents are in on it too. At one time or another, they are all heard to remark: "We spend the first few years trying to get our kids to walk and talk and then spend the rest of our lives trying to get them to sit down and shut up!"

Why does this matter to us as creative beings? Because a creative mindset is basically not reinforced during our entire childhood. Yes, there are creative moments in school, but usually even arts classes are structured so that every kid is doing what they're supposed to and working toward a common goal. Even creative writing assignments will be graded low if they're too creative or unexpectedly different. The creative mindset exists naturally in a child. Despite the efforts of our parents and teachers, it is somewhat exercised during our lives. All we need to do is to break through a few barriers to let it loose in a semicontrolled way. Those barriers would be things like preconceived negative outcomes, fear of attempting something without knowing in advance how well you'll do, and an inability to allow a chaotic, unstructured mental opening to exist. If we believe (as I do) that our true creative ability is childlike and not organized, wouldn't it be nice if we could organize that creative information? Say yes.

This is where knowledge can really help. For instance, a knowledge of music theory could instantly help you try the simple 4/4 idea you just came up with in 7/8 time, or in the relative minor of the original key, or diatonically harmonized, or as a call-and-answer counterpoint. These suggestions are not necessarily creative, since they involve using techniques—finite, defineable, teachable techniques— to enhance a creative theme. If you know all your basic theory, it won't take more than a few minutes to try those techniques on any riff. It will be a lot quicker than stumbling around for days and then realizing later that the second section you've been slaving over is just the first section in a different key. By the way, that happens all the time with new writers.

What about ear training? How could that possibly help you write tunes? Well, if your ear is in good shape, you could analyze every song on the radio as it's playing. I'm not suggesting anything that is beyond working musician-level expertise. If you work on your ear training and learn some basics of structure, you can sit down and create at least a Nashville-style chart of the tune, where the actual key is not defined but the chords are given (e.g., 1, 4, 5 or I, IV, V). Obviously, you don't have to have perfect pitch to begin analyzing most all of the music in the popular spectrum. And if you get in the habit of analyzing music, you'll find yourself getting out of creative ruts by using thought processes like: "Let's see, I've tried all the normal keys for the bridge of this song. Hmm . . . maybe I could find a way to modulate a tri-tone away like that neat tune I heard in the background of that airline commercial." Thus you can be inspired by a particular technique used on someone's work and apply it to your own idea without being derivative.

Creative moments happen more and more easily with experience. As you realize that you've stumbled upon a useable idea, record it in some fashion so that you'll be able to remember it for later. I find that some ideas really draw me in and invite me to work on them for a long time. On the other hand, it's perfectly cool to hit on a riff that you know will inspire some future work, and to record it and get back to the project at hand. Use calligraphy, tablature, sequences, or actual cassette recordings, or whatever medium you have to keep track of your idea. Just be sure to play it enough times to remember the feeling that you had when it first fell under your fingers. That's important, because it will lead to the next section.

How do you get to the next section when all you've got is a single idea? One way is to play the original idea until you can play it without stumbling. Next, try to play it when it's fresh, not after you've just repeated it a thousand times. Then, try to remember the original feeling you had when you created the idea. Get in the same frame of mind as the music you want to create. If it's rhythmic, move with it; if it's melodic, make it expressive; if it's angry, then feel it that way.

After the last note of the idea has been played, keep your eyes closed, keep the rhythm in your body, and listen to what your mind adds to what you just played. It sounds crazy, but your brain has definitely written the next section or at least the beginning of the next section already; it's just up to you to listen for it. It may be so faint that you can't hear it. It may be that all you hear after the last note of your riff is "I'll never be able to finish this tune!" If that happens, then just concentrate the way you do when someone is talking during a movie. You can either listen to them or tune them out and focus on the movie. Your subconscious composer is always there writing stuff that nobody usually listens to.

The most mysterious thing is learning to listen to your own subconscious ideas. Once you realize that you can do it, everything will seem simple in comparison. Then you'll have to worry about which ideas you like better, or which ones fit the bill, or maybe how to stop seeing so many possibilities. You know those 3-D posters where you have to stare for a long time with your eyes focused on a different plane than the paper? I think they make a good comparison to composing. Everyone will think you're weird if you concentrate on one picture long enough to see the dimension that's hidden there—just like your friends and family will think you're weird if you zone out to find the musical possibilities of a theme. And, like writing, once you figure out how to see what's hidden beneath the surface, you'll find it quicker and easier to do the next time. Finally, there will always be some people with short attention spans who just won't be able to see what's there. Make sure you're not one of them.

Creative Room

The creative process is one of life's great mysteries as well as an important issue for all musicians. I like to write about it, since it sometimes decides how far we go with our music. Someone who finds a way to be creative almost on command will obviously have many opportunities to find his niche in life. On the other hand, musicians who are not prolifically creative may have to persevere longer to find a great gig. All in all, many things decide our direction, but if you look at any successful group, you will always find at least one person at its core to whom creativity comes easily.

Since I wrote about the creative process from the composer's angle in November's column, it may seem as if I'm covering familiar ground here. The truth is, 1 can't stop wondering why so many people become defeated by the challenge of writing and improvising. That's why I'm really harping on this one for a few sessions.

Let's say that you've stumbled across this riff that you think is cool, and after trying some of the ideas that I suggested last month, you still don't know what to do with it. Or perhaps you're playing your guitar right before you call it a night, and you develop what might be a good idea, but you don't have enough time to finish it. In both cases, you should find a way to record the idea and come back to it later when you have a different perspective, or when you can spend some more time with it. By committing it to tape, you'll free up mental space for other ideas. Even though some musicians can switch channels quickly, moving back and forth between two (or more) ideas, most seem to do better with some creative room.

How should you record your ideas? In my opinion, it's best to have a simple, quick system. Obviously, it would be great to have a score and a sequence of every idea, but there are some problems with that approach; if you make a big production of a rough concept, you'll tend to delay the recording of it until you think it's good enough or finished enough to warrant the effort. It's best to treat all your ideas as possibilities and not as nearly-finished works. That means recording them quickly.

I use a simple hand-held recorder—no wires or plugs. I just set it down and turn it on. First, I'll play the riff in the tempo that I imagine would fit it best. Then, if the part is complex, I'll play it again at a slower tempo with an audible click track or beat. This makes it much easier to relearn the piece if I don't return to it right away. Once again, human nature plays a part in this: If I'm listening to old ideas on tape and the phrasing or notes are hard to pick out, then I won't be able to see the fingering positions in my mind, and it will be much harder to remember that part. That could lead to a subconscious desire to pass over the idea for one that's more clearly recorded.

Often, the clicks will be nothing more than my foot tapping on the floor next to the recorder. When I'm on the road, I record my axe acoustically, with the recorder two feet from the guitar. (A note: If you use a recorder with variable playback speed, it's helpful to play a long tuning note before an example for when you go back to relearn it.)

I've worked with and seen many guitarists who prefer to write ideas down. I imagine Scott Henderson, Trevor Rabin, John McLaughlin, Frank Gambale, or Steve Vai literally writing down their ideas based on the ease that they have with the written medium. One advantage to this is that you have the opportunity to put in all the right fingerings, even if you're just writing in tablature. Once again, though, whatever you do must be made easy for you to review in the future, so that you won't put it off or avoid it.

Now let's go forward in time and imagine you have a number of ideas on tape. Where do you start to put them together? To my way of thinking, I write the music that inspires me. In other words, if it doesn't really move me, I'm not going to spend any time on it. Whatever style you write in, you must develop a sense of what's good enough to keep and what needs to be trashed. If the idea of trashing anything you create upsets you, just recategorize the "not so good ideas" as "things to work on later . . . much later."

When it comes to judging which ideas to work on, I find it's best to have audio recordings, especially if it's been a while since I last played the pieces in question. This gives me a chance to develop an objective feeling as each idea is heard. Naturally, you'll have to play make-believe, since the quick recordings won't sound like a record.

But if all the ideas are recorded similarly, the good ones will jump out. Remember that, just as when taking a test, your first reaction is probably the most correct. (At this point, I could probably write an entire sidebar about how weird it is to use the word "correct" in the context of judging art in general, but instead I'll just ask you to let me get away with it.) Keep the ideas you really love and put the rest away. Or better yet, trash them. "What? Did he say 'trash them'?"

Yes, for a few good reasons. At some point you have to start making decisions, because the more creative you get, the more possibilities you'll end up seeing. Part of being creative involves constantly saying "no, that's not good enough" in order to give yourself the creative room to work on your best efforts. Another reason to trash ideas is to raise your standards: The less hesitation there is to try something better, the greater the chance you'll come up with something better.

So, experiment, document, evaluate, sort out the best, and develop them. Sound easy enough? Give yourself some creative room by moving out the ideas that don't make the cut, and it will be.

Speed Bumps

I'm not sure if it's politically correct to talk about technique these days, but let's do it anyway. I'd like to see if there are any readers who would give me some feedback for a simple experiment. I've always said that improving technique is one of the easiest things about playing guitar, and therefore I haven't considered it much of a challenge. But I'm noticing that almost any skill that requires some level of repetition and concentration is becoming more scarce. Basic technique for the guitar seems to be a stumbling block for the vast majority of guitarists.

Probably the hardest part about doing this is knowing when you're playing a part perfectly in time. Usually, people will say that they're able to play a scale or riff at a certain tempo. But when I listen to them play at the speed they think yields perfect timing, I'm convinced that they can't hear their own mistakes. The real challenge is to know when you're able to play cleanly and perfectly, even if the tempo is one note per minute. Obviously I'm slightly exaggerating, but the tempo for playing perfectly should be as slow as it takes.

Here, then, are four steps toward improving technique.

Step One: Find Your Baseline Tempo

I want you to play this exercise shown below slowly and learn it so that you don't have to look at it on paper. It's just a pattern up and a scale down, so it shouldn't take too long to learn. Get a metronome, sequencer, or drum machine to help you gauge the beats per minute (bpm). Find the bpm at which you can play the example *perfectly*, with absolutely every note in time. Naturally, this will be a slower tempo than you are normally capable of playing. Write down the number of bpm, and we'll call this the baseline tempo.

Step Two: Increase Your Speed Incrementally

Play this example and alternate it with some scales or modes that you already know. Do this for five minutes at the baseline tempo, trying to play each note perfectly in time. Every five minutes, move up one bpm, and repeat what you just did.

Step Three: Go For The Max

After 30 minutes of this, you should have moved up five bpm from your baseline tempo. Remember what was the fastest tempo at which you could play all the notes perfectly. It very well may be your original baseline tempo, but usually you'll hit a higher number in a repetition like this. Take the fastest perfect tempo and add 10 percent (e.g., if the tempo is 85 bpm, you would add 8.5 to get 93.5 bpm). Round off the increased number to the nearest setting that your machine will display.

Step Four: Let It Rip
Play the exercise and alternate with scales at this increased tempo for five minutes, regardless of whether or not you are making mistakes. Turn off the time-keeping device, and play the exercise one time perfectly, probably at a slower tempo. Now, do whatever you want until tomorrow.

Tomorrow, start at step one and establish a baseline tempo. If you haven't warmed up very much, the tempo could be the same or even slower than the day before, so try to do some normal warm up each day. Repeat all the steps and write down the results each day for at least 10 days. If this doesn't increase your speed and accuracy, reread the instructions and try again. Good luck.

Cleaning Up Your Act, Part 1

Little distractions can take our attention away from things that are more important. If you're making your Great Musical Statement, but the sound isn't very good, or there's a lot of hum or buzz coming from the speakers, you and your listeners won't be able to fully enjoy the music. And while age-old advice tells us that a good song will shine through even a bad mix, much of your music's best details will be lost on your listeners. That's because it's hard to focus on the important aspects of music when you're being disturbed by little annoyances.

When it comes to cleaning up your guitar sound, there are a number of factors worth considering. This month, we'll focus on fine tuning your guitar's performance to minimize noise and improve pitch and tone.

To start with, play your guitar without an amp and see where the strings buzz and "fret out." By "fret out," I'm referring to where a string touches a fret other than the one you've chosen to play, thereby killing the string's sustain. Before you make adjustments to the action, look down the fingerboard and compare its straightness to the string just above it. Because of parallax and the fact that the strings don't have exactly the same angle as the fingerboard, all you're looking for is a noticeable dip or arch on the fingerboard. Don't worry if you find one; as you'll see, it's easy to fix.

In general, the truss rod in the neck fights the pulling action of the strings. Simply try to figure out who's winning the tug-of-war: the strings or the truss rod. If the neck has a hump in the middle, you need to loosen the truss rod and let the force of the strings pull it back straight. When adjusting the truss rod, it helps to push the neck in the direction you want it to go. To do this requires four hands or some padded support blocks and two hands, whichever is easier to round up. Remember the general rule for tightening and loosening a screw—"right tight, left loose"? That's what you're doing to the truss rod when you turn it.

Now that all the guitar repairmen are writing letters about a certain columnist over-simplifying a neck adjustment, let's move on. If your open strings are buzzing and your neck is straight, don't panic. The lower strings typically will buzz a little in the open position if you hit them hard. If your playing style involves really whacking the strings constantly, you might want to consider playing heavier low strings or (gasp) raising the action. Before you actually do that, try putting your left hand near the headstock and gently bending the neck in a slight bow while you pick the open strings. Does that help eliminate the buzz? If so, then try adding a tiny bit of bow in your neck adjustment or raising your bridge slightly. If the bending experiment doesn't help the buzz, then it's probably the frets nearest the nut. If this is the case, raise the nut by the smallest amount possible. That usually means placing a shim, which could be a single sliver of paper, under the nut. Use as much finesse as possible when trying to free up the nut to change the height; they can crack. I like to break the glue joint loose by sliding it sideways before I attempt to lift it up.

Incidentally, this is a great time to put on new strings and adjust the intonation. We'll do it using the simplest method: play the 12th-fret open harmonic and compare the pitch with that of the fingered 12th-fret nonharmonic note. Using the harmonic as a reference, decide whether the fretted note is higher or lower in pitch. (Sometimes it helps to bend the fretted note slightly to see if it gets closer in pitch.) If the fretted note is too high, adjust the bridge saddle away from the nut; this makes the string longer and, in doing so, lowers the pitch. If the fretted note sounds flat compared to the harmonic, then raise the pitch by shortening the string—that is, by moving the saddle closer to the nut. While you're doing this, remember that the force with which you push down on the fretted note is a factor, and it should approximate the force that you normally use. Also, note that we're accepting the angle at which the nut is filed and using it as a reference point to define the harmonic pitch. Just be aware that a really good guitar repair person can change the nut fulcrum points enough to actually improve the pitch in the first few frets.

Try some of these suggestions, and next month we'll look at ways to clean up your amp sound.

Cleaning Up Your Act Part 2

Last month we looked at some ways to clean up the sound originating from your guitar. This month, we'll play with some ways to eliminate some of the unwanted noises that occur when you plug in.

It's one of those dichotomies of the music business: There's a million-dollar studio, with trained engineers flown in from other continents to record a guitarist, and the producer has just instructed everyone to make it sound more trashy. These episodes do happen with some regularity, and as electric guitarists, we totally understand the fact that some dirt in the sound—maybe a little 60-cycle amp buzz—makes the world go around for some styles of music. So let's concentrate on cleaning up that other stuff that nobody really wants.

Starting with buzzes. Turn up the amp and guitar volume. Alternate between touching your guitar strings and keeping your hands off the guitar's metal parts. If there's more noise when you don't touch the guitar, then your strings are connected to the audio ground. That's the way I like it, but there are some circumstances in which the hum would suddenly be much louder. For example, let's say you've got a lot of gain and compression on your sound, and at a soft section of the song, you play a ringing natural harmonic. The moment you pull your left hand away to let the strings ring, the hum comes through loud and clear. Flipping the polarity/ground switch on the back of your amp has no effect. What to do?

I once faced this situation during a session; the hum would pop in whenever I momentarily let go of the strings. It was bothering me, so I came up with a strange solution: I took a long wire with alligator clips at both ends and clipped one end to a convenient metal piece on the bridge. I doubled up a flat sheet of aluminum foil, clipped the other alligator clip to it, and set the foil on the floor. Living in the South, it's pretty normal to be in the studio barefoot, so I simply stepped on the aluminum foil. Suddenly, no more hum problems.

I tried a similar solution for my classical electric guitar. As you know, a classical guitar has three nylon strings, which don't conduct electricity or help a grounding problem. What I did was to attach a small metallic patch where my right forearm braced the body of the guitar, then hooked that to the audio ground on the guitar's electronics. That way, the amount of hum wouldn't suddenly increase as I moved to the all nylon strings. My latest classical guitars, by Buscarino, are quiet enough that they don't need that fix, but I would certainly keep it in mind for some other well-known brands in a critical recording situation. (Note that while both of these examples work well in the studio, you might have some trouble putting them to use in a live situation.)

Many studios these days revolve around some kind of computer sequencing, sampling, or direct recording. One bad side effect of computers is that they radiate noise that our guitar pickups can hear. Even on a humbucking pickup, being too close to a computer or many micropressors will give an annoying buzzing noise. Fluorescent lamps can sometimes do the same thing, to a lesser degree. If you hear some buzz, turn off the lights for a second to see if that makes a difference. If so, change your position to find a place in the room where the buzz is minimal.

One nice studio trick is to record a direct line at the same time that the amp is being recorded. Usually, the direct box will have a polarity or ground lift switch. Always take the time to find the quietest setting, since the direct box will probably be boosted and leveled by a compressor in order to be usable. Any buzz in your sound will get worse as you add compression and high end, so check the sound with exaggerated level and high-end EQ to hear the results of your ground lift.

Another way to clean up some raunchy guitar parts is to artificially mute some of the strings. Let's say you're playing a slide part using just two strings, and the amp is cranked in order to get that sweet sound. Problem is, the other strings aren't always muted, and they ring open and spoil the sound somewhat. Just grab something soft, like tissue, paper towel, or cloth, and weave it between the strings that you're not going to be playing. Now you can concentrate on getting good tone and vibrato, *and* stay in tune without worrying about the other strings running away.

There is yet another type of noise pollution that can come up and surprise you. I was recently doing a Deep Purple overdub at my studio. The song had a click track, and I was listening through the control room speakers while I recorded a bunch of electric guitars over one section. Later, at the big studio with the band, we decided to have total silence while these guitars rang out one chord to end a section. Was I ever embarrassed to find that just enough click track had leaked through the pickups to make my efforts unusable! To prevent this from happening, either turn the speakers down very low while you record, or use headphones when recording a crucially bare section. This can still happen when you record acoustic guitars, even with headphones on. If you can't turn down the headphones enough to stop the click from bleeding into the mic, you can try what I call a "smart" click track. Using MIDI volume, or actual recorded volume, have the click track get much quieter in the sections where the guitar is ringing, and louder in the busy or strumming parts.

Lastly, and no less important to your sound, get a really good guitar cord. They aren't all the same, and the cheap ones are bad enough to affect your sound and even be microphonic on the high end. Triple-shielded cords are the best way to go. Also, if you're using a tuner inline, find another way to feed it while you're in the studio. To get the strongest signal, you want the shortest length of the best cord going straight into your amp, and some tuners do produce insertion loss.

I hope this helps, or at least gives you some ideas. Good luck!

The Well-Tempered Communicator

What's the mark of a much-liked musician? I'm not sure if it's any one thing, but you can bet that they've figured out how to communicate in a positive way. As you may already know, there are musicians who don't really need others to interact with them; however, the majority of us do. I think about this a lot in my Deep Purple gig, since I'm surrounded by guys who habitually put things very well when they talk. By that I mean that they get the point across with no misunderstanding and no offense. My friend Sterling, at E. Ball, is the same way. Nobody ever has a doubt about what he just said, and nobody feels bad about himself if he offers a few suggestions. Actually, nearly everyone on my list of legendary creative forces in music has the ability to be tactful and clear, to make their criticisms and observations "well put."

When does this quality come into play in a typical musician's life? Actually, having this ability will help you every minute that you speak to anyone about anything. Let's look at a few ways you can improve your communication skills.

1. Say What You Know

Let's assume you finally have some money to buy an amp, and you're ready to make a purchase. Walking into a music store, you tag the first salesperson you spot and say, "Uh . . . do you guys have any amps?" This will usually be the signal for the salesperson to start playing 20 questions with you, as he attempts to determine your needs. More than likely he'll leave you standing there on your own when a phone call comes in.

Now, instead of taking that approach, try simply stating what you already know: "Hi, I'm ready to buy an amp today. I'm looking for a tube combo with one 12" speaker for less than a grand out the door." Watch how much more attention you'll get when the salesperson knows that you're ready to deal and that you have an idea of what you want.

2. Give Positive Advice

You've heard of constructive criticism? Here's how to put it into practice. Let's say you're writing a song with a friend, and you express your displeasure over the way the chorus makes you feel by saying, "This song bites!" That will usually throw a bucket of water on any creative fire that was burning. Instead, tell him: "I feel a little uncomfortable every time we do the chorus. I think maybe it could use a chord change or something. What do you think?" Now you've made your point, but you've also introduced a positive direction by suggesting something like a chord change. Plus, you've involved your friend in the solution by asking him what he thinks. I know this is basic stuff, but I wouldn't be writing about it if it wasn't such a widespread problem.

3. Take The Kinder Tack

Good communication abilities are an obvious talent of every busy sideman. I know for a fact that strong people skills can put a good musician in a first-call category, ahead of other possibly more skilled players. Don't believe me? Imagine Mr. Hotshot showing up to back up a famous singer. When asked to play the second guitar parts, Mr. Hotshot becomes offended and says, "That's ridiculous! I always play from the first guitar book!" On the other hand, Mr. Gets-the-gig simply says, "Sure, let's give it a try. It might be fun to play the second guitar part for a change of pace." In short, he communicates the fact that he would normally get the first book without coming off like a total jerk. And he'll probably stay on that leader's first-call list because he didn't intimidate or correct him.

4. Make Your Needs Known

Let's say your agent calls or faxes a tour proposal, and you look it over and find some problems with the routing. You could start with the time-honored observation, "This tour looks like it was booked by a monkey throwing darts at a map!" On the other hand, you could make the conversation productive by saying: "Thanks for sending me the tentative dates. It looks like we won't be able to make that jump between Denver and Houston overnight without a travel day. Can you switch something around with that fact in mind?" Now the agent knows your limitations with the trip. Even if you've told him before how many miles you're willing to travel on gig days, you've alerted him to the fact that it needs to be changed, and you've done it in a way that won't leave him cursing you after the phone is hung up.

The main reason that groups break up is because of personality problems that get in the way of their communication about music. If a group ever makes good music together, that's a sign that musical chemistry is there. Many bands exist and even thrive when some members disagree about basic issues outside of the music. Usually you'll find that they've learned to communicate without the use of insulting comments or overtones. Obviously, it's best when everybody loves everybody else and peace and harmony prevail. Until you find that situation, say what you mean and temper it with good intentions.

Opportunities

Two things happened this week that provided the inspiration for my column. First, I just finished some gigs with Manuel Barrueco, an absolutely brilliant classical guitarist. We played together during a tour of solo guitarists called The Guitar Summit. I was on one leg of the tour and made friends with all the guys playing, but Manuel agreed to play on a duet that I had the music for, and he just nailed it perfectly. Along that tour, I just missed meeting up with Michael Hedges again, and found a note from him suggesting we get together sometime. Since he didn't leave his number, I assigned someone the task of tracking him down and telling him of a project idea I had. Then I went back to the chaos of my normal life.

As you know by now, I'll never get the chance to get together with Michael again. Hearing of his death was the other event that happened this week, and it shocked me into thinking about many things. One of the first reactions I had was that he had a family with kids, and what could ever make it be okay for them? Then came the guilt for not following up on his invitation. This subsided a little when I remembered that I did extend an invitation to him to play on a compilation project I've been working on, through all the proper channels. Even so, I never did get to spend more than a few minutes one on one with him, though I was relaxed in the knowledge that we would get together again.

In my situation, I really do not have time to pursue every single opportunity that comes along. But I sure do consider each and every one that I'm made aware of. Then I thought of the concept of new projects, and all the aspects you have to consider when tackling them. Determination is one quality that's necessary in attempting any new project. When you become determined to see an idea through to its conclusion, that idea doesn't get lost in the shuffle of other good ideas that never went anywhere.

For example, pick a popular song that you think is pretty well-written. You can probably come up with ways that the song could be changed or improved, say to better fit the singer's range or style. A song as it exists is just one version of millions of possibilities. In those millions of possibilities, wouldn't there be some that we would like better?

To me, the answer is yes. Any worthwhile effort could always be changed and improved in some way. There are always an untold number of ways we can push our efforts. Most important, though, someone actually made the decision to call it complete and deliver it to the listeners' ears.

You don't have to know beyond a shadow of a doubt that the time is perfect to actually try something. You just try it with your best efforts. Determination can see you through to the end. Your best effort at the time will get you more recognition than if you just imagined how great your work would be someday when the time was absolutely right.

How does this relate to my gig with Manuel, the classical guitarist? Well, before I actually did these shows, my mind was reluctant. I was feeling that the time just wasn't right, and that we should wait until we could arrange things better. But despite the slightly uncomfortable feeling of not getting in much rehearsal, I agreed to try it since I thought so highly of Manuel. As it turned out, we were limited to one rehearsal the day before the first show. And you know what? We were pleased with the fact that we had to stretch a little and make do with some simplifying. At the last minute, because we didn't seem to have much time, I successfully got Dave LaRue to accompany us on some pieces, and it really made the show better. In retrospect, a little action netted us more results than a lot of hedging, and I can see that pattern in every successful moment of my past.

Maybe you too can try that musical idea that you're not too sure the band will like. Maybe try playing in front of an audience (if you've ever dreamed of doing that), or playing solo. You might surprise yourself, and I guarantee you will become a better player as a result. Maybe actually do some of the things you've always wanted to do but never quite started. Record that home-brewed CD or start that garage band or write that song. It doesn't have to be perfect. In fact, it never can be.

Hey, why not try something with a musical friend in honor of Michael? He was always generous with his praise, so try telling your friend some of the things you really like about him and his music. Try just once treating him like it's the last time you'll see each other. You might see enough good come of it to make it a habit.

Losing Through Intimidation

Before the cassette with the song idea even finishes, someone in the group announces that it's not going to work. Sound familiar? Or "I'm not going to play that. I hate it." I once observed a musician turn around that kind of attitude by replying, "Oh, I guess we'll tell the record company president that his favorite song idea isn't going to be on the album." Seriously, even though this scenario is common in many bands, it kills part of the creative process.

You've heard the term "designed by committee," right? Well, in a way, writing and arranging music in a band is similar. Imagine a bunch of people sitting around a table at an automobile design center. If one person in the group has some power and is dominating, there will be more "yes men" and fewer candid opinions. Compare that picture to another company where the people are free to give their ideas and honest opinions. I guarantee that the second company will be more innovative, and if the rest of that company is allowed to have natural creative input, it will build a better car.

Let's break down an example. Assume a guitarist brings in some idea first. (I never said I was completely unbiased.) We'll call him the rhythm guitarist. Now, we could pretty well bet that he thinks the idea is worth working on, or else he wouldn't have brought it in. So the rhythm guitarist plays through his chord sequence and then looks up to see what everyone thinks. Let's see what the reaction would be like in three different scenarios.

In a domineering situation, the other (lead) guitarist might say that there's nothing worth working on simply because he didn't come up with the idea. In that case, he might intimidate the others from saying that they "thought it was a good place to start, and it's too early to judge it." The other band members may have noticed that it doesn't pay to cross the domineering one in the band because it results in huge power plays and threats. The other band members may be extremely creative on their own, but with this situation they're not effective as a unit because the free exchange of thoughts isn't possible.

What about in a politically correct climate? In this case, after the guitarist plays his idea, everyone says it sounds great. Does this idea really sound great? No, it could use some work to flow better, a key change for the singer, and some original twists thrown in by the band. Why aren't they suggesting those things? Because everyone is intimidated by the notion of rocking the boat. This is exactly what I saw while watching a TV show where a jury of various listeners decide whether a music video is cool or not.

In actuality, the idea of offending anyone or being self conscious keeps them proclaiming that basically whatever is put in front of them is cool. That's not a bad attitude for someone put in an awkward position, but creative musicians need to rise above that fear. In fact, the old joke "it had a good beat, I could dance to it" came from a TV show where a few people would be asked to rate a new song as it was played. That quote was the only politically correct response, given the pressure of being instant critics. The point of this example is that creative input will invariably involve some changes, and you need a climate that allows that to be easily expressed.

For the third scenario, imagine that the idea has just been played. The drummer says, "Let's try that with a little bit of a shuffle beat to move it along." The lead guitarist says, "I'd like to try answering those vocal lines with a short guitar riff." The singer says, "I agree about the key change, but can we look at those lyric ideas again?"

By now you may have guessed that this is the preferred scenario. Everyone immediately has opinions that will make the song idea better, and they're not afraid to voice them. Also, no one feels that he has to pretend it's a great song for the band as it stands. It needs work to fit in this band. With everyone feeling free to at least try all the suggestions, the stage is set for some inspiring things to happen. The guitarist who brought the idea was not belittled even though everyone had some kind of change in mind. In this imaginary band, there is enough good chemistry that something good will eventually come of almost every starting idea, whether it ends up being used or not.

You've probably seen all three types of groups, but perhaps you didn't think about it at the time. I know that I've seen and been part of all three many times over the years. The freedom to make suggestions is important enough to be the cornerstone of any successful group.

Influences

The first guitar hero that I got to meet was Jimmy Page. After a Zeppelin concert, we slipped backstage, hoping for a glimpse at best. I walked up to him, awestruck, and after a brief question-and-answer session that consisted of one question, I learned what kind of strings he used. The questions that I really wondered about never got asked: "How did you come up with all those great riffs? Who did you listen to? Who were your influences?"

Most guitarists have a pretty short list of other guitarists that they would list as influences. I think the reason for that is the conception that influences must come from similar musical styles in order to be influences. In other words, people expect your outside musical influences to be obvious stylistic ones. But what if your influences came from instruments other than guitar? What if they came from other musicians outside of the category in which the record stores file your recent purchases?

First of all, when you open up the horizons of who can teach you, the choices grow astronomically. Good music is just good music, and it is found everywhere, not just in the top ten. In order to really stretch out and find more music that speaks to their souls, many people find specialty record shops, internet connections, and audiophile magazines to offer good tips on finding interesting music.

For example, if you were to listen to and learn some keyboard compositions, you would quickly start to think in bigger intervalic jumps on the fretboard. You'd also get frustrated by the fact that we can't play as many notes at once on a guitar as on a keyboard, but you can still squeeze out some parts that will be musical on the guitar. Sax solos are many jazz guitarists' favorite to transcribe. Why? Probably because of the jazz influence, the natural phrasing of an instrument that requires breathing pauses, the bending of notes, and the similar stage. I have gotten a lot out of musical studies for the violin, cello, and clavier by J.S. Bach. Since Bach was writing in the Heavy Baroque/Metal style anyway, the stuff works great on guitar while getting away from the blues clichés.

What about influences that just don't even seem to make sense at first? Like people who don't play in the style that you are mostly accustomed to playing? Or writers of books or magazine articles? For instance, I find great inspirations from guitarists who I don't emulate stylistically. I sound different from Dweezil Zappa, but the fact that he, like his dad, totally follows his creative instinct makes him an influence. I understand that cartoonist Gary Larson is a guitarist, but

I've never heard him play. He's been an influence by showing how entertaining a little juxtaposition can be, as you've seen in his *Far Side* cartoons, which show animals smoking cigarettes and talking like people. Maybe I wouldn't have talked the guys in the Dregs into playing a bluegrass tune at the Montreaux Jazz Festival without having been influenced by that juxtaposition.

Let's talk about a way to be influenced by your guitar hero of the moment. Say you've just gone to see him or her play. See if you can be inspired by more than the notes or the riffs. Think back to the inspiring moments and try to find a trend. Maybe the guitarist was very melodic and expressive. Don't necessarily copy his solos (although that might not be a bad place to start if he really was melodic), but try to be influenced by the impact expressive melodies can have on an audience. For another guitarist who you listen to, you might deduce that every solo is explosive and relies on sheer attitude to come across. The message might be that some music can support that kind of attitude very well, as opposed to transcribing those particular moments of angst.

Vocalists can help us to believe that a simple melody can exist over a complex musical structure. Like I mentioned about saxophones and other horns, the need to take a breath leads toward the kind of phrasing that feels natural. Our fingers would do well to practice taking little pauses, if only as an exercise. Listen to some of the subtle ornamentation of some basic melodies sung by an Irish folk or traditional Indian singer to get a feel of how much can be done without going off the deep end.

Once again, when you open yourself up, you can be influenced by everything that you contact—filtered, of course, through your frame of reference. If your frame of reference is a positive, can-do attitude, then seeing a guy struggle to get up a wheelchair ramp with no assistance will make you see your difficulty with a song project as something you can overcome. Seeing a little kid who believes an unused cardboard box is a spaceship might wake you up to the fact that somewhere inside you have the same level of creative imagination that could be used to find a more innovative approach. Witnessing the birth and end of a storm cloud could show you that immense power and the anticipation of it is very exciting. It's all there, we just need to realize it.

By the way, Jimmy Page is always listed as one of my influences, and not just as a musical influence. On whatever scale a particular gig involves, every time someone stops me on my way out the door to ask a question or get an autograph, it's nice to remember how Page handled a nervous, excited fan.

Maintaining a Positive Point of View

Have you ever played for people and felt it went poorly, but the audience thought it sounded good? Playing for a group of family members doesn't count, because they'll always tell you that you sound fine. Or, on the other hand, have you ever seen someone perform when he was obviously drunk? Most likely, he thought it was going great, but your ears told a different story. Whose point of view is right?

Many would argue that the majority opinion rules; others may believe that music can't be judged at all. The assertion that I want to discuss is the belief that your experience (or anyone else's) is unique—even when many people experience the same event. That element of human nature may make it difficult to find a corroborative eyewitness for an event, but in a concert, musicians need that diversity of opinion to support a variety of music.

Why does this matter? As musicians, we want to express ourselves. But we also want to do it well. If we write a song, play for others, arrange for a group, or teach students, we want to be good at it. If we do those things and believe that we're doing them poorly, we'll eventually lose interest in pursuing further projects. However, if we do what we like to do, and we feel we're doing a good job, then we're more likely to feel confident and excited about the next project.

For example, let's say one evening I wrote a tune. After listening to it the next day, I don't think it's very good, because the B section doesn't do anything for me. Should I try to convince myself that it really does sound good, so that I won't be discouraged from writing another song? No. In this example, the writing is something that can continually evolve until the song is published. (Even then you can still improve on it.)

In this case, the solution is to smile and tell yourself that after all the work you did yesterday, you may have a usable A section, and then get to work on a different approach for the B section. After all, painters have to constantly stand back from their work, to separate the parts of the painting that need work from the parts that please them. Writing music is something that works well spread out over a bit of time. You have to rejoice over the bits of music that truly please you, and fix the ones that don't. Otherwise, you might get discouraged and throw away the whole thing because part of it doesn't work.

For another example, imagine that you have been looking forward to a band gig at a party. Your band hasn't played much in front of people, but you've been rehearsing well. Everyone is excited just knowing that soon he'll be playing in front of a real crowd. Finally, it's Saturday night at the party, and there are a few problems: the vocal mics are producing a lot of feedback, the band plays everything too fast, and you can't seem to come up with a great-sounding solo in any tune.

Since there was no wild applause like there is when a band plays a party in the movies, you assume that the gig was a bomb. But before you get depressed, hold on a minute.

First, if the gig was no good, why did two other people ask you if you could play for their events? Second, you just got a great lesson about placing the P.A. *behind* the singers. You also learned that next time, taking an extra second before each song to feel the correct tempo might be a good idea. And the age-old lesson that it's harder to play a solo freely when you're put on the spot has hit home, lending credence to practicing more than you think you need to before performing live. All in all, you're much better off because of the experience. This point of view will help you.

I don't believe everything is always beautiful, no matter what. Yes, I do believe that all things fit together, whether they seem good or bad. But I don't think we should tell ourselves that something is great when we easily could do much better. So here's one of the catches in my theory of maintaining a positive point of view: Everything you tell yourself has to be true. Face facts, but face them in a constructive way.

I'll give a personal example. I had just finished a show and I was feeling bad because several solos that normally come easily were just plain lousy. Rather than tell myself that it sounded okay, like my friends would tell me, I'm going to look at it differently. I'm going to go to my room and work harder to play freely over those solo sections, and I'll bet it will be a lot better the next night. I think it's more productive to do something to make yourself better than to wish a mediocre result was a great result. To me, that works. The self-affirmation comes from getting better, noticeably better. There really is some beauty in every failure we experience. It gives us the opportunity to notice (and improve) an area we may have ignored.

By the way, the example that I gave about playing a bad solo has happened often, of course. The interesting thing is that someone usually mentions it was their favorite gig. Like I said, it's all in your point of view.

Preparing for the Beyond
Things to Do to Get Ready for a Tour

Here I am, a passenger on the second flight of the trip, in my fourth year with the group, on my way to the first gig of the world tour for our new album. The flight attendant just came by to pull down my shade and was surprised to find someone still awake. I'm still on a musician's schedule, and we normally go to the gig around the time it gets dark, so I'm still up and running. I have no idea what it will be like in Istanbul, my first stop. Let me correct that: the little computer on which I'm typing this column has just given me a brief history of the city. What sticks out is that Istanbul has been established for 10 times longer than the U.S., and is one of the major producers of motion pictures.

Now that you've gotten a mental picture of where I'm at, let's talk about the things a band would normally do to get ready for a tour. The first thing after getting the product ready (in this case, I'm referring to the CD, as opposed to the band) is to book some gigs. What is normally a straightforward process becomes significantly more complicated as more people are involved. When you add in the problems of jumping across borders and continents, things take a while to confirm. This means that you can't control exactly how things will wind up, and you can't plan much other stuff. For me, it comes down to keeping huge blocks of time available for touring, and then scrambling to be ready when there is some time available for other projects or vacations. People I meet who are on the Internet often know the band's tour schedule before I do. This is usually caused by a few unconfirmed gigs holding up the release of the official schedule, while the Internet version of the tour is posted and then changes.

The next thing is to round up the usual suspects, or hire a crew. In this case, I'm told that only a light man is new. Considering that we had a lot of time recording and being off, that's pretty good. Touring techs usually stay on the road by hopping on the next tour after one finishes. Still, it means that the new guy is going to have to learn his cues at a full-blown rehearsal. I think that's one of the reasons we're renting a large venue for four days in our first city. It also gives the returning crew and band a chance to work in the typical stage environment. The band can typically help a new (or existing) light man or sound man to program his computer by giving him advance notice of what songs will be on the list. However, on this tour, there's no chance of that, since we like a lot of the songs from the new album, and we'll try them all before we decide which ones stay on the live list.

I'm always grabbing stuff from my little rack of effects, since I have a few favorite sounds on my rack gear that work for solo gigs, trio gigs, seminars, real recording studios, and home recording. So when a tour starts, I have to check my equipment and reinstall whatever effects I've borrowed since the last tour leg.

In this case, the equipment was leaving a couple of weeks before me, hinting at some of the potential problems of transporting it. Most of the time, it seems that the stuff flies on the same airline as us. But they still like to have it early for the first gig, even if it goes by air. Normally, I would check the cases and spare supplies, but for this tour, Skoots or Charlie do that, because the heavy equipment is far away in storage.

We check for basic tools, soldering and electrical parts, tubes, and spare chords. We have spare amps set up for a quick change if one fails. That may have been inspired by the time the local stage crew accidentally sent 480 volts to the 120 bus. We also bring voltage meters, power screwdrivers, strings, and, of course, black duct tape. (By the way, I was recently fixing an air conditioner duct. I used some of that tape around the joint of the air duct and it worked great. Hmmm...maybe what the roadies told me about the origin of rock and roll tape isn't 100 percent accurate.)

Luckily, since there's no image ordeal, packing for the trip is a breeze. But after being amazed at some of the weather extremes we hit last time, you better believe that I checked out the expected temperatures. For an international trip, I bring a lot of my own reading material, because other than newspapers, there's not much stuff in English to choose from. Prescription items, some legal herbs, and supplements aren't readily available, so you've got to bring them. Ditto for favorite brands of consumable items like deodorant or shampoo.

Once the band is together, it's time to finalize the songs on the master list. Usually, we like to have a lot more available that can be played in any one night. The mix will probably include about four new album songs, two from the last album, three oldies other than those we played last time, and the classic hits. This is a good time to throw in my preferences, since set lists often look the same from night to night. So I have no problem pushing hard for the ones that I enjoy the most.

Also, we'll be coming up with definite endings for those pesky fadeouts that seem fine on record but don't work so well live. The normal fix is to come up with an ending based on an existing riff or theme fragment. We'll have to consider tempos, types of feels, and the singing style of each tune that goes on the list. For example, we can't have five in a row that Ian will be screaming at the top of his range, nor can we put two together with a similar feel.

Well, it looks like we're ready to land at the starting point of this tour. I'm ready to get started.

Another World
The Twists and Bends of Life on the Road

Hurtling. That's what Ian Gillian calls it, as we rocket at 135 miles per hour down the Autobahn. In Germany, the fast lane makes American highways seem like residential streets. But it's not all pedal-to-the-metal cruising. Just when you get comfortable with the fact that you're covering more than two miles a minute, you have to slam on the brakes to avoid a truck that suddenly pulls out at 50 mph to pass a slower vehicle.

Having been away from the familiarity of home and family for more than a month, I've become numb to all the endless traveling I've been doing, whether it's been by bus, limo, plane, taxi, escalator, elevator, or foot. So why does hurtling down the Autobahn capture my complete attention? I think it's because the outcome doesn't seem such a sure bet. The driver is good, but he can't control the other vehicles. Also, I think the constant shift between full acceleration and abrupt braking tends to keep me from dozing off.

By now, you're probably thinking I should make a musical analogy. Well, it *is* true that a predictable solo that doesn't change pace much is pretty uninspiring, right? The same is true for speech patterns. A monotone delivery never holds people's interest. A lack of variety is boring, but zooming along the Autobahn, constantly changing speed and sometimes suddenly stopping, can be downright exciting. I think the same applies to music.

This leg of the tour has already landed us in seven countries, and it's getting hard to remember where I am, what day it is, what home is like. But we have had some great musical experiences, and we're really playing well together. When you're on the road, you exist solely for your gigs, and you do everything you can to make them great. Almost every night, we talk about the show after we're done playing. It's not a structured meeting, but we all offer our feedback on how it went. Still, there's no getting around the fact that I'm only onstage 10 to 12 hours a week; that's only about six percent of the time that I'm on the road.

I think most people have no idea that musicians spend inordinate amounts of time to spend a few hours doing what they love. I constantly see groups paying to play for a shot at opening a festival or arena gig. It all seems natural when you're doing what you love, but the more you have to compromise, the quicker it wears thin.

What do I mean by compromise? Well, for example, if you're party-ing a lot, chances are you're not practicing much. And, as most of us know, guitarists really do need to practice, as you'll notice when it's time to step up for a solo. For me, it's a serious compromise if I feel distracted during a solo.

Distractions include worrying about equipment, sound tuning, song arrangement, and technique. My roadie, Skoots, always takes care of the first three, but I'm in charge of the playing. I know I've said this before, but it really helps to practice beyond the point of being able to play the obvious parts at home. It's best to feel free enough with your technique to be able to experiment without having to worry about whether you can play something or not while you're on stage. Of course, you *will* still make mistakes, but that's all part of improv-isation. If your technique is good, you'll be more confident, and a small mistake is never a big deal—unless, of course, you notice that three camcorders have been snuck in, and every note you're playing will be analyzed and bootlegged later.

Since this is a rambling column (no editor's wisecracks, please), I'll share an interesting bootlegging story. Last tour, a guy showed me a thick book filled with descriptions of different Deep Purple bootlegs. There were between 450 and 500 listed. So when I'm relaxing and improvising that magical moment, I try not to think that I'm usually not playing just for ticket holders at the show.

I just remembered another interesting tidbit. The stadium concert in Chile that I wrote about last year is in a television advertisement. The ad features horrible things that have been captured on tape, and sup-posedly banned from TV. However, for a certain price, plus an exor-bitantly high shipping and handling charge, you can own a tape of the horrific scenes. In this case, the camera crews captured the seething mass of out-of-control kids who literally climbed barbed wire fences to get into the stadium and onto the field. In the process, the light tower toppled over onto the crowd below.

Well, you can save money and experience that moment for free if you look carefully at the TV ad for the right second or two. There are probably lots of different tapes like this for sale, so I doubt if this one is still being advertised, or if it has any of the gig on it, but many of us in the band and crew confirmed that it was our gig.

Well, there's one thing that *does* hold this column together: It's all been written on the road, while touring with the band. And it's another world.

Trial by Fire

It all sounded good at first: I would finish a fairly long leg of a Deep Purple tour, my trio would go out and play a couple of interesting gigs, and then I would go back out with Purple. It was only after the trio gigs were booked that we found out our drummer, Van, wouldn't be able to make it. He had a summer-long tour in Europe to do, and he couldn't get off long enough to do the gigs with the trio.

Our bassist, Dave LaRue, suggested Dave DiCenso, a drummer who teaches, records, and plays around the Berklee School of Music. As the gigs approached, Dave L., in his usual organizational style, sent Dave D. a list of songs that we would choose from. He also e-mailed them to me so I could look them over while I was in Europe, and also be prepared. After my long tour-leg with Purple was over, Dave L. arranged to come over and review some of our stuff to make sure we both remembered it.

As Dave L. and I ran over our songs, I started wondering how Dave D. would be able to jump in cold and play all of this. Having not played this stuff in months, it seemed obvious that we had a lot of kicks, cues, and weird parts to brush up on. Then I remembered that Van Romaine had virtually jumped in cold when he joined the band, and that made me stop worrying. But then I remembered that Dave D. was subbing for a couple of gigs only; I started worrying again. After all, how much preparation would most guys do for a couple of fill-in dates?

A couple of flights later, we were driving to the first gig for soundcheck. At soundcheck we left an empty space in the middle of the stage for Dave D. to set his drums on. We waited and waited, but there was no sign of Dave D. My worrying returned.

Whenever a band makes musical changes, or hasn't played in a while, they rationalize that they can fix all their unresolved problems at soundcheck. Even though it's really just wishful thinking to believe that much rehearsal is ever possible during a typical soundcheck, it remains a traditional rabbit's foot for musicians to depend on. In other words, it's like studying for the final exam on the bus the morning of the test.

Well, well, well. No drummer for soundcheck; no rehearsal. This could turn out pretty ugly. I ask the chef in the kitchen what he recommends for someone that will be developing an ulcer shortly. He looks at me with the most deadpan expression and then resumes chopping vegetables. I settle on some rice mixture and soon Dave DiCenso arrives.

He looks remarkably calm, and directs the setup while quickly grabbing something to eat. Dave L. and I hit the hotel for a quick shower and return for the gig. When we walk in, Dave D. is lying down resting. I am amazed at how cool he is under the circumstances. He gets up and asks about the order of tunes and then arranges a thick pile of papers. He has actually charted out the whole list of songs from which that we chose the set. I ask him how he could have done all that while he was doing all these other gigs, and he remarked in a casual way that it was no problem, adding, "Thanks a lot for that measure of 19 in the fifth tune." So he even had a sense of humor about it. Dave L. and I start to talk about tempos, and it turns out that Dave D. has even written down the exact tempos on his charts; I'm really starting to feel like an amateur at a convention for the pros.

Minutes later, we're onstage, and it all becomes clear. These two guys named Dave are playing great and making it easy for me. This must be one of the reasons that we're supposed to be able to read charts. Dave D. goes the whole set without making a noticeable. Amazing. I'm very impressed and inspired, not just by our temporary drummer, but by the amount of trouble everyone in the organization went through to make a couple of gigs happen. I also can't help but admire our full-time drummer, Van, who never hesitated to recommend a top-notch fill-in. We can't really imagine traveling or playing without Van, and it showed his ever-generous nature to insist that we do the gig even if it meant working with a substitute.

So the lesson here is that it's the people you work with who make this line of work so interesting. Never miss a chance to be inspired by them.

Band Chemistry
The Importance of the Right Personality Mix

Well, here we are, enjoying a 15-hour drive to a far-flung but likable province of Canada. Some days are easy, and some days are just long. I figure that we average about 9 1/2 hours a week onstage, out of a total of 168. To do this for a living, you should really love it. I guess I really do, even though I'd like to have complete control over the scheduling.

Anyway, one thing that really stands out during this trip is how the band stays in good humor throughout the day (and night) of traveling. I'll elaborate on this because I think it's important.

In order to take a band through touring, whether or not it's on a big scale, you have to face living in each other's space. Things you'd never think would even be mentioned become an issue. Think about how long it can take to get a group of five to 10 people to decide where and when to eat, and then imagine doing it several times a day for months on end. Every aspect of touring—when to meet, when to soundcheck, what to play, how long to play, what direction to take the song, and on and on—has to be dealt with as a group.

Yet despite the constant consulting and approval-gathering, I am convinced that to have a good band you must have a mixture of personality types. They can't all be super laid back, or else no one will have the intensity to look at what might be. Then again, they can't all be intense and stressed out, or no one will be able to show the others how to enjoy the success of the moment. Somewhere the issue of chemistry comes up.

Imagine that a prospective manager approaches your new group and offers to pay for a CD recording project if the band signs a contract. In a balanced group, you might have one person jumping for the first available pen, another who wants to get advice from a lawyer, another pointing out that recording a CD is an inexpensive proposition anyway, and yet another wondering why a band would even need to sign a contract for more than the money advanced.

I think the enthusiastic one would play a part by keeping the energy up, and inspiring the band to take risks. The one who wants to get a lawyer first would represent the voice of caution and conventional wisdom. The guy who points out that homespun CDs can be great or horrible is being helpful by reminding the others that there are no guarantees of success just because certain words are spoken. The member who questions necessity of a contract for more than the funds borrowed could be the creative thinker who challenges the status quo.

Say your band is just beginning to work on its image in the very early stages of its existence. It sounds nice if everyone wants exactly the same thing, and the end product should be something on which everyone agrees. But in the process of deciding what the group stands for, there should be an intense discussion with many different points of view in the mix. Inevitably, there will be some swaying, and maybe some compromise. But in the end everyone should feel a power greater than any individual idea at work.

It's the same when you jam or write songs. Everyone should have different ideas to contribute (or you all need to listen to different radio stations or albums until you do). That's when the innovative stuff comes in. The drums and bass might start a simple beat centered on one note, but then the keys add a moving chord pattern over the top. The guitar changes the feel by accenting the upbeats and suggesting a riff every fourth bar. Then the singer surprises everyone by singing in the relative minor. By sticking with it and experimenting with open minds, the entire band ends up loving the final product. That's the result of good chemistry.

Speaking of bands with good chemistry, I finally got to check out the entire Dream Theater show here in Canada, and the band is performing great. When there were a few minor scheduling disputes early in their tour, all of the principals worked it out without drama. Someone from the crew was passing around a quote from singer Henry Rollins that said something like, "Listen to your stage manager and crew, since they know the full deal about each gig. They've been there all day, and will be there for hours after you're gone." I'm paraphrasing from memory, but the idea was for the artists to just pay attention and work within the parameters. All the crews were working together with amazing teamwork, and it was contagious.

In the case of Dream Theater, you probably won't find a more capable guitarist than John Petrucci. DT seems to have worked together enough to be comfortable for a pretty long haul. Every band has its differences, but I get the feeling that the members of Dream Theater have put the music at the top of their priority list. For them, music is the main ingredient in a proven chemical formula.

There It Is
Ready to Practice on a Moment's Notice

This time, the importance of my electric guitar's design became obvious.

The overhead compartments of the 747 I was on were the small, flat type that just won't fit most guitars. I was glad to have my guitar with me on this flight, since it meant being able to whip it out during the long drive to and from the airport. If I carry my guitar in a flight case, it usually gets stuck in a truck, luggage van, or the trunk of another vehicle. With my carry-on bag, it's easy to hold my guitar while I sit like an otherwise unoccupied commuter vegetable.

How much does it matter? With millions of TV channels, the Internet, and ever-increasing demands on our schedules, a lack of time becomes the problem. People are more attracted to doing creative things on computers than to spending nine hours a day practicing guitar. I guess most people don't realize that anyone who claims to spend nine hours a day practicing is literally living in another world. The truth is, you can get a lot from the guitar if you have regular time with it. A series of short practice sessions over the course of a day will give amazing results, especially when working on memorizing music or technical exercises. However, those results will be very different from the depth that can be achieved with longer, uninterrupted practice sessions. You will usually get more out of touch with reality during a long practice session—and for creativity, that's not a bad thing.

If there were a guitar sitting there ready to be played every time you had at least 20 minutes before your next scheduled event, would you practice more? Yeah, you would. You'd look at your watch and realize that you've got a few minutes, then you'd think about eating or making a phone call, then you'd look over on the wall and say, "There it is. I might as well practice."

You might ask, "Why should practicing be such a big deal when I can already play the main guitar parts for all of the pop songs on the radio?" Well, when you play someone else's parts, you're not going through all the steps that were involved with that final guitar part. It may have involved writing several other sections, then editing them out, then revising the part for the producer who insisted on simplifying the background. So while it's good to learn other guitarists' recordings (especially for ear training), you need time to discover the instrument on your own terms.

The more you know, and the more with which you're comfortable, the less likely you are to make excuses like, "Well, that part doesn't work because it sounds too self-indulgent." What you really mean is, "I can't play that! No way! You're putting me on the spot!"

Am I actually suggesting that you leave your guitar just sitting out all the time? Well, if it would make you practice a few times more a week, then wouldn't the little bit of dust that might settle on it from staying out of its case be worth it?

Leaving my guitar out works for me, although it wouldn't be too much trouble to get an easy-access case for it. I get my best results when I can't talk on the phone, watch TV, or eat without seeing the guitar. Sounds crazy, maybe, but out of sight, out of mind. Everyone says I'm out of my mind, yet my guitar is in plain sight. Hmmm.

One thing I've noticed about practicing in small segments through-out the day is that it takes less time to warm up when I return to the guitar, even when it's hours later. By doing this, you can play with less effort right away, and that usually sparks some inspiration. It's always difficult to come up with ideas out of the blue when you're struggling just to get your fingers to follow simple commands because it's been a long time since you last played.

So grab your most comfortable axe, clean up the neck, and make sure it has good strings. Tune it up, and put it in plain sight. Next time you've got a few minutes before some scheduled event takes you away, you'll look over in the corner and say, "There it is."

Creating Space
News Flash! Not Playing Can Help Your Playing!

It seems that the headlines for everything in today's newspapers are worded to read the exact opposite of conventional wisdom. You know: "Red Meat Found to Inhibit Cancer." "Parents Do Not Affect Kids' Behavior." "Exercise Makes You Die Younger." I guess the bottom line is that these headlines catch your attention.

I saw one that actually gave me some hope: "Study Finds that Brain Cells Keep Growing As We Age." Doesn't sound that impressive to you? Well, considering that we supposedly lose IQ as we age, and brain cells by the day, this one is worth believing. If exercise keeps our bodies working well, and stimulating the brain gets those new cells to work, we have no reason to fear tomorrow.

How does this relate to music? Well, look at my headline: "Not Playing Can Help Your Playing!" Like many of these headlines, it's misleading, but it contains a thread of truth. In all dynamic art, having small pauses, or anticipations, can lead to a more dramatic conclusion. So in effect, if you stop playing long enough to have pauses between phrases, you can come off as more musical.

For example, say you're playing a song with steady rhythm all the way through. Sometimes there is just no substitute for the raw energy of a constant pounding rhythm, right? I agree, but what if just once in a while, you left out one or two eighth notes in the rhythm, and let that become a different pattern for a portion of the song? Or how about skipping 1 and 3 of every bar so that you play an eighth-note pattern that becomes: rest, strum, strum, strum, rest, strum, strum, strum. That gives the bass drum and the bass more punch, because you're creating a hole for them to fill. I could be mistaken, but it seems that Charlie Watts of the Stones always leaves out the backbeat from his hi-hat pattern for his snare to be heard stronger. That's another pattern that would be cool to try instead of constant eighths: strum, strum, rest, strum, strum, and repeat.

I know I've harped on this before, but paring down your guitar part to nothing, or to a very minimal pattern, when someone else is soloing will really help. For one thing, it will give them a chance to be heard. For another, it will give them some rhythmic freedom with which to experiment. The sound man will also appreciate that your rhythm parts are not the same volume as your lead lines or solos.

One way that I bring it down when someone else is soloing is by playing a sparse pattern, mostly rests, with one or two strings muted by my right hand holding them to a very short duration. Also, I frequently use one of my single-coil pickups in situations like these. By having one of the single-coil pickups mounted far from the strings, I have minimal magnetic interference as well as an automatic gain decrease. Why do I want a gain decrease? Well, if I'm normally playing with a lot of distortion and I want to bring it down to a clearer, easily controlled signal, I just select my number one single coil. It gives me instant control and increased treble to counter the effects of rolling off the volume with my pinkie finger. It saves having a night/day transition of a channel switch on your amp.

What if you're playing an intense tune and are worried about bringing down the energy level too much? Think about this for a minute. You may be cutting down in volume, but the soloist is being brought to the audience's attention to make up for the fact that you're not playing as much. Sometimes soloists (particularly keyboards) have an extra reserve of volume, or at least the soundman will bring them up if they need it. All in all, if you do you your part to create some space, the soloist will be heard without the soundman having to do anything. Just letting the soloist be heard will add some variety to the tune. That's always a good thing, no matter what style you're into.

Patience?
Attitudes Make All the Difference

On the left side of the stage, the rhythm guitarist glares in the general direction of the other guitarist in the group, Mr. Big Shot, over on the right. The guy on the left side is thinking that the guy on the right only cares about himself to play so loudly and drown him out. "He even missed the cue where I play a riff for him to join in on the last tune!" says Lefty. "How can he be such a jerk to not care if he hears me?"

Meanwhile, on the right side of the stage, the other guitarist is taking every opportunity to try to catch the eye of the monitor engineer, who is busy with a technical problem: The drummer can hear only the rhythm guitar, not his usual mix. The guitarist on the right side is definitely catching some weird vibes from over on the left, but says to himself, "I can deal with all of Lefty's problems later, but right now I have to get my monitor mix right. All I can hear at the moment is my own guitar drowning everyone else out!"

Does this sound like something that might happen to you? Obviously, we've all been on both sides of a similar fence. Life in general seems to reward patience when dealing with others. The problem is that if you're a highly charged, passionate person of the musical persuasion, in the heat of the moment patience may seem like a dimly remembered lecture from childhood. You might think to yourself, "Patience? Man, I play intense music. I can't do it by sitting around trying to be patient!" Yes, but. . . .

What if the way we played was different from the way we deal with each other? What if people were more complicated than a typical seven-note scale structure?

You know that I've said this in this column before: People's attitudes make all the difference. How about a retake of the scene I just described? Lefty notices that Righty just missed Lefty's cue. The only explanation seems to be that Righty didn't hear him. Lefty says to his roadie, "Make sure that Righty's monitor mix is okay. He just missed a cue that he normally nails perfectly."

The roadie goes over to the monitor man, who is freaking because the more he turns up Lefty's guitar for Righty's mix, the more the drummer screams about too much guitar in his monitor. Obviously, some wires are crossed, and there are now three guys trying to trace the problem so everyone can get the correct mix. Righty can't hear anyone because of his incorrect monitor mix, and quickly comes over to Lefty at the end of the tune, since there have been no bad vibes thrown. Righty says, "Hey man, I couldn't hear your cue at all, they're having problems with the monitors. I'll just unplug mine until they sort it out. Let's keep good eye contact in the meantime since it'll be harder to hear each other."

It's no big deal. The problem is getting fixed, and nobody is freaking out. That's because Lefty paused to give Righty the benefit of the doubt. That patience is also what kept the guitarists from jumping up and down screaming at the monitor man, calling him all kinds of names. It turns out that some cords got switched during the set change by one of the house helpers who needed to run some wires. The monitor man was justifiably baffled, since it really was okay just before the band came onstage. The house helper unplugged the cords to run his wires under them, then accidentally plugged them back in wrong.

Managers, record companies, and booking agents are the only ones in the music industry who seem to never be on the receiving end of patience. Kidding aside, it's a pretty thankless job, since musicians have difficulty relating to business realities. Like, "What do you mean it's a 16-hour drive, again?" "What you mean they're trying to promote it the best they can?" Or, "You should have been able to turn our club act into an arena attraction by now! It's been months!"

Be patient in times of stress. Not blind, not ineffective, but patient. It works for all aspects of our musical and personal lives. And yes, I do try to heed my own advice. Have a good one.

Looking Back
Impression from a Year Gone By

It's late December 1998 as I write this, and at the end of every year, I try to look back and get some perspective. Actually, it would be nice if I could have perspective all the time. Anyway, as I look back on 1998, I have seen some new things and relearned some old things.

New things? The word "privacy" has apparently been removed from the dictionary after some rock stars got personal videos stolen and distributed absolutely worldwide on the Net. On the other hand, the Internet seems to be the most logical medium for artists to have contact with the public. That actually represents progress, although there is still no easy way to find music without knowing the name of the group. Anybody want to be the next Internet billionaire and start a music search engine that will find music by theme, lyrics, style, or description? I'll help if anybody has a few spare years to spend on it.

The press (led by international TV networks like CNN) appears to be incredibly powerful, and influences the entire world, as evidenced by the Iraq conflict and the White House stuff. My theory that the publicity team for the movie *Wag The Dog* hired Linda Tripp to tape Monica was never proved, so I can't ever write that exposé for the *Enquirer*.

The world has gotten smaller. This past year I spent a very large number of days in foreign countries, and people outside the U.S. all watch (and criticize) what the U.S. is doing. At the moment we seem to still lead the world in computer design, software, and entertainment like music and movies. So once again, if you're a working musician, you're helping the trade deficit.

Relearning old lessons? I guess the first one that comes to mind is that musicians have a pretty tough time if they're not following the latest trend. Actually, that's nothing new, but now it seems more difficult for bands and artists to get established through radio airplay. If it's not on a video clip, in current rotation, it's not on the radio playlist.

Also, I learned that good memories come from working with good people. Since I've been gone a lot with Deep Purple, I've really missed the occasional mini-tours that my trio used to do. As I'm writing this, I have been working on some new arrangements with Dave LaRue, and it's really fantastic to hear someone who is awesome after you've been apart for a while.

One of my best friends told me to always tell your family how you feel about them (assuming that it's a good feeling), because you may not always have them around (meaning that they may die, especially parents as they get older). In musical terms, I now never miss a moment to tell my bandmates when I am amazed by them, since these are the moments to remember.

How about straight music lessons? I've learned that the only way to be truly relaxed onstage is to have my chops up and running for sure. When I have just the slightest bit of anxiety about a difficult section coming up, it ruins some of the appeal of the experience. So the best drug of all is that seductive aura of the music itself, which can be reached only by not thinking at all of your fingers, body, arrangement, or tempo. Not thinking of distracting stuff is easy if the technique is there. The beginning of each tour leg gives you an intense adrenaline rush as you are moved by the fresh appeal of music, and the end of each leg finds you totally relaxed and pushing the envelope as technique gets a kind of a workout different from practicing at home.

Another noticeable trend is that I'm a little more likely to play right in the pocket of the beat after another year of working with Ian [Gillan] and Roger [Glover] in the DP rhythm section. Those guys lay it down so solid that it's helped me pinpoint the types of situations that make me rush a bit. Also, the time I've spent jamming with Jon Lord (keyboards) has given me more confidence to develop unorthodox motifs in a solo. He is a master of improvisation and is very relaxed about it. He is totally engrossed in his music when he takes off and can improvise multi-thematic works of art on the spot. It's like being in continuing education courses for me.

Each year seems to be going by quickly, and 1998 really did. One theory I read basically said that if time seems to go by too quickly, you're working too hard. The guy who came up with that theory wasn't a musician, and doesn't know that you get wrapped up in your work if you love it. And I do.

Roadies to Glory
The Do's and Don't's of Playing as an Opening Act

Just got back from a tour leg with my trio. At every stop across 8,000 miles of highway we had one, or sometimes two, opening acts. The thing is, every one of these acts was good. Actually, really good. The fact that good players seem to be alive and well is something that I will write more about soon. But on the subject of opening shows: People have asked why we picked a certain opening act, unaware that the people in the venue office, in all likelihood, did the picking. To give you some more enlightenment on factors that matter in live performance, what are some of the do's and don'ts of playing as an opening act? I've talked about this a little bit before, but I get asked a lot, so here it goes: Don't worry about the money; you're doing it to play in front of a different, and hopefully larger, audience. And by the way, there's very little to worry about in the money department, since there's usually very little money. If you play to hundreds of people from your area that have never heard you, and you impress and move them . . . well, they might pay a cover charge to see you across town next weekend.

Do be on time with your equipment to set up. It doesn't happen very often, but we do see a club manager get mighty upset when the opening act is late and doors open late. It follows that the less time a club is open, the less time there is for the club owner to make money.

Don't expect a full sound check, catered dressing room, equal time onstage, etc. All it takes is one problem to blow away your chances of sound checking before doors. Oh yeah, that one problem may not even be the headliner's fault, like a sound system failure. Dressing room? Many clubs have only one, and the headliner crew has driven a lot longer than you, a lot more days than you, and is a little crankier than you. The dressing room sofa might be the only place a weary roadie can catch a quick nap. It's best for you to arrive pretty much ready to go. Actually, it's easier for the opening act, since they can show up an hour before doors, play a short set, and tear down straight out the back door, all in two or three hours. Contrast this to the headline crew, who has to load a lot of stuff in at 2:00 p.m. and load out at 2:00 a.m., many times to drive all night. You really don't want to hassle them about the dressing room.

Do be yourself. Choose the songs that you love. Don't try to second guess the crowd. Yes, a crowd will applaud an opening act that is in the exact same vein as the headliner if they're good. But they will applaud very loudly if the opener is original and somewhat unexpected . . . and good. The best way, always, is to start with what you love—there's a better chance that you'll work on it more. My opinion is that all things being equal, you would do well to not come off exactly like the following group. Try not to copy their style, but dig deep for your own.

Don't plan on borrowing equipment from the band already set up onstage. I will gladly let anyone borrow my stuff if they're in a bind, but most musicians, and especially roadies, feel a little uneasy when someone asks. Drummers have it the worst, since a basher can dent the heads, change hardware settings, and strip threads on adjustments. What if you borrowed a bass amp, changed the settings, and the tech forgot to check one of the knobs before the headliner went on? Do you think that tech would get a smile from the bass player? Can you see that the roadies are a big part of the picture when it comes to being an opening act? Yes, the audience is essentially your employer but, in a more realistic light, you better get along with the road crew and the venue's stage manager if you want to have a good recommendation.

Do be polite. No matter how awesome you are, if you piss off the stage manager, that pretty much takes you out of the future running at that location. I don't think anyone should burn bridges; besides, it violates the Golden Rule.

Do end on time. This is the one that most acts ignore. They're playing well, the audience is happy and applauding every song. Why quit just because some jerk is pointing at the clock and getting all upset? Because that's part of being a professional, doing what you said you would do. Remember what I said about the stage manager and the crew who have to keep the show on schedule? Do you really want to make them mad? Try just five minutes overtime and see how smiley their faces get as you unwittingly cut 15-20% from their time to re-mike the drums and front line. By using five minutes of their time, they can't go to the cooler for a drink, or hit the bathroom before they get on their work stations for the next act. Nobody cares what a genius you are when you go overtime on a tight show; everyone who is aware that you're not quitting on time can't help but feel like you're being disrespectful.

If you didn't bring your own soundman or lightman, **do** thank the people that did it for you. Chances are good that they didn't get anything extra for doing your set. All in all, just do your best to treat everyone with respect. When you're finally a big star, you might just want to keep that habit, since trends have a way of changing. Start right now being amazed at how hard everybody works to be in show business, and you will have a better chance of remembering that all your life.

Can "Live" Survive?
Starting a Band and Playing in Public

People often ask me about the prospects of a career in music, especially playing in a band. It has never been easy to start a band and take it from the beginning all the way to where it has a life of its own. Nowadays, with the hundreds of channels on TV, virtual reality games, high-tech arcades, and the millions of web sites offering instant gratification, it's even harder to compete. But in the subculture to which our band plays, there are noticeably more people and fantastic local groups to support the show. Things are pretty good, but according to the reduction of rock industry record sales, they're supposed to be much worse.

What got me really thinking about all this was the fact that everywhere we went, there was at least a very good band based in the area willing to open those shows. In some cases, the performer had other gigs later that night at different clubs in town. How can there be so many polished, experienced performers if nobody supports live music? To me, the answer is that people do support it; it's some of the demographics that may have changed.

For instance, the faddish, pop groups have simply changed from groups that play instruments to groups that are more likely to be choreographed and sing. Country music has become the place to sell a song that would have been considered A.O.R. (album-oriented radio), or even pop, a dozen years ago. R&B has moved a little closer to rap, and vice-versa. So the Spice Girls, country, and rap artists do have the huge numbers that MTV rock bands had at one time. But rock and jazz still exist even if they're not heavily endorsed by TV and radio. There is still a core following that doesn't seem to be going away like it's supposed to. Good news for a lot of us guitar players.

Here are some suggestions for improving the chances of starting a good group:

1. The best time to experiment is when you don't have to worry about paying the rent. If you're lucky enough to have parents or someone support you as a teenager or young adult, that's the best time to explore your musical boundaries. Let's face it, if you're already married with kids, your first priority has to be feeding the family, right? That means less opportunity to travel, rehearse, or try non-paying musical gigs. I know plenty of people who play in good bands while having a day job, but they're hard-working, organized folks by nature. If you're interested in music now, and you're a teenager at home, you've got the opportunity of a lifetime without realizing it: 52 weekends a year with very little to do in the way of chores, bill paying, house maintenance, tax record keeping, business correspondence, or baby-sitting. As you grow up, you'll realize how nice that could be.

2. Open your mind to any musician that you have time to play with. One very good group that I know combined a classical guitar with an oboe, another has an accordion and a slide electric, another has a jazz banjo, bass, and electronic drums. The best way to get yourself into the right frame of mind to do this is to realize that everyone has a unique perspective on life and can teach you something from his or her experience. Believe in that—it's true.

3. Consider making changes early on if there is no positive chemistry. You have to give yourself enough time with a person(s) to see what develops, but you have to cut your losses and move on if your heart tells you that there is just no inspiration there. Oddly enough, the more good that you can see in someone, the more good you can pull out of that person by really telling them the good things that you notice. It sounds really simple, but it works. With all that, if things just don't feel good ever, change them so that you're not trapped in a negative cloud that will suck away your creativity and energy.

By the way, if you do have to make a change, give the others as much respect and dignity as you can possibly manage. Saying "You guys suck! I'm outta here!" creates more bad energy without solving anything. You might try saying, "I'm really glad that we got together and played these last two weeks. You have a great technique on the drums, too. I honestly am looking for a different type of sound than what we always seem to gravitate to, so I'll be working with some others for a while. I hope that this won't stop us from being friends." It will make you stronger as well as allowing them some honor. Speak nothing but the truth, so that your words will stand up. At the same time, speak nothing but the positive, especially when you have to break away from other musicians. Musicians need to be pretty sensitive to see the subtle possibilities hidden in an idea. Remember that every time you speak.

4. Play in front of people on a regular basis. I always say this, because it's important. When you are working for a deadline, it gives you more incentive to put things together and try them-like, "We've got to get this tune in shape so that we can play it at that party on Saturday." Plan some type of performance, even if it's for a dozen people, at least twice a month. I promise that's an important one.

5. Repay your parents and friends for helping you out. You have no idea what a sacrifice your parents make when they let you use the garage or basement to rehearse in. It means the neighbors will be a little more grumpy at them, your parents won't be able to relax in their own place during that time, they'll be dodging equipment to find their stuff, and they may have to talk the police out of issuing a noise citation at some point. What about friends that help you lug the stuff to and from auditions, parties, and rehearsals? Well, if you're a musician, you're broke, and you probably can't repay them. Still, just acknowledging their help will put things in a more respectable light. I still wonder if I thanked people enough along the way.

Live music will survive all this millennium stuff, mainly because live musicians might be the only source of entertainment that doesn't have embedded Y2K chips (just kidding!). Like I said at first, it seems that there are quite a few good musicians going for it, but there's always room for more people to express themselves with music. Give it a try.

Trading Solos
A Time to be Heard and a Time to Back Off

Can you pass and shoot well? In basketball, it matters. Even the best shooters pass to team members who are in a better position to score. Every guitarist has opportunities to trade off with other players in the band, even if they aren't necessarily guitar players. If you have a trio, you might trade solos against a melody or theme that surrounds the solo. Or you might trade off with a vocalist, with the solo complementing the vocals as a melodic element. If you play with other guitarists, though, you will certainly want to have some skill at trading off riffs.

Are there any rules? No. But I have some suggestions based on years of playing and listening. In the case of two soloists (again, not necessarily both guitarists) it doesn't matter how great one of them is if he walks all over the other. If player "A" is wailing and then drowns out player "B" when it's his turn, the effect is frustrating to the audience. Nobody wants to see that kind of thing. People would rather see two people working together making something out of nothing than one person obviously trying to smother the other.

First suggestion: Let the other person be heard. Simple? Yes. Common? No. Guitarists need to realize that the soundman can't usually react fast enough to turn you up or down at precisely the moment you start and stop a solo. Every musician should spend some time being a soundman to understand that. Yes, some people can react pretty quickly, but think about typical, realistic situations. You really need to create your own dynamics. I know, I know, it's hard with distortion and all that, but it can be done. For starters, try totally not playing while the other(s) are soloing. That gives several benefits to the soundman. By not playing, you give him time to make adjustments to the next soloist's volume while actually being able to hear which soloist it is. Also, it removes the guitar frequencies from the mix, making it much easier to hear the other even without making a level change on the mixing board. Stopping totally is kind of extreme, but it makes a dramatic impact. In a lot of cases, we can improve on that idea.

A more skillful approach is to drastically reduce the density of what you're playing while the other person is wailing. Some techniques to master are:

1. Muting with the right hand. This will shorten the notes and leave some spaces to hear other things in the mix. If you're using a lot of distortion, the muting can have the effect of adding low end unless you reduce the gain somewhat. So practice instantly jumping to a muted sound while you bring the guitar volume down a bit. If you're using natural distortion, you can easily take some of the extreme thickness away by bringing the guitar from 10 to, say, 7 on the volume knob. Get to know what degree of turning works by feel, not by looking at the knob.

2. Make the sound thinner, with less apparent volume. This is closely related to what I just said, because you will probably use the volume control on the guitar. But to really make the sound seem less loud, you will probably have to bring the knob from 10 to something like 3 or 4. The reason is that the amp starts clipping and overloading after a typical setting of 3, for instance, and every increase after that adds distortion, texture, harmonics, and all the stuff that guitarists want. Obviously, if you have a channel-switching amp, just try switching channels. But beware that you will still most likely have to turn down the guitar, since you've probably got the clean channel set up for a final volume similar to that on the high gain channel. In this case, bringing the guitar down to 7 or 8 might fill the bill.

3. Change to a different pickup. This is easy on my guitars, since I have a couple of single-coil pickups set pretty far from the strings that are excellent for chopping some intensity, while keeping the original amp distortion available to make the change a little smoother. But, Strat players can have one pickup backed off just for that reason, and Les Paul players can preset the other pickup volume control down so that when they just flip the switch, they have less gain and a different sound.

4. Roll some high end off. That's right. I'm actually suggesting the use of the vestigial tone control on many guitars. It works wonders when you need the thickness of the guitar without the screech. This application works best when the other soloist's sound needs either the high-end range, such as a violin, or a full range vocal mic. It's fairly subtle on some guitars, but try turning some high end down, then bring it back in when you solo. This will make your solo stand out a lot more, because other sounds are heard when you have the tone down. I was pretty concerned about getting the tone control values right on my axes, since it's an important tool.

5. Play less. Try making a brief accent on the 1 of every bar as your first experiment. The drums are probably whacking out the back-beats, so don't worry about the 2 and 4. Just try it while someone else is featured. You can try keeping a large part of your solo sound intact if you play brief accents only. Imagine that you're adding a little bit of salt and pepper with your accents. A little does good, too much ruins it.

Remember that there is a time to be heard and a time to back off. If you do it right, the soundman won't be so tempted to turn you down while the other player is featured.

Talkin' Trash
Under the Hot Spotlight, It's Not All Raves and Praise

"If you can't stand the heat, get out of the kitchen!"

I did. Twice. But that kitchen turned out to be the closest thing to my goal of playing music. What's wrong with finding a way to cool down the kitchen and stay there, too?

If you're not following this, I can understand. But there is a point. That is, why does being a musician mean that you're automatically supposed to get and give callused, negative press for ridiculous or non-existent reasons? How does this apply to you? Haven't you ever judged some other musician on sketchy or flimsy evidence?

We often jump to the worst, or most accepted, conclusion when in actual fact we don't know the whole story. Example: Your drummer is late for rehearsal and you know that he stayed out last night with some rowdy friends. Everyone assumes that he's hung over and couldn't get it together. In reality, it turns out that he was picking up the equipment van from the shop because nobody else could be reached by phone when the shop called. Since it's Friday afternoon, if he hadn't done it right then, the band wouldn't have had transport to the out-of-town gig tomorrow. Meanwhile, as the drummer rushes to write the check to pay for the van repair, everyone else in the band is talking trash about him.

How about another universal classic: You and your group go out to hear another band playing nearby. The guitarist is doing pretty well and is featured in quite a few solos, which sound good. For some reason, one of your group starts the discussion with something like, "Who the heck does he think he is, acting so cool like that? He must have a huge ego to take so many solos, too!" Meanwhile, in the reality room, this guitarist has just had a conversation with his own band in which he's been told, "Look, man, you're playing great. But you've got to get more confident and make your solos a little longer. Don't be afraid, just step out in front a little more and try it." So the shy guitarist, trying to please his band with his efforts, takes their advice, not realizing that your group is talking trash about him for just trying his best.

Bad press can be born for many reasons, often independently of the unlucky recipient. Just today, I found out that I was advertised to appear in two different cities at music stores. The problem with that is that I had other, actual bookings for every bit of time available.

Also, nobody told me about these appearances until after the ad appeared. Result? Nobody takes responsibility; everyone assumes, or is told, that I canceled. Imagine what you would do after waiting around for someone to show up after scheduling your day around that event, then hearing that they just decided not to show up? Instant bad press.

The same thing happens if the stage manager cuts off the opening band when they go overtime: "The headliners are jerks." Also, people regularly have asked me why I canceled a gig here or there. In reality, the agents send out feelers for a possible run to many venues. These are not to be advertised, because they are not yet confirmed. What if a risk-taking promoter decides to advertise in an upcoming print ad (usually a lot cheaper for him than short-notice radio ads), and lists the artist and a play date? Sometimes they even sell tickets on it. A few days later, the agent calls back and says he can't make the run work out, for logistical reasons, and the promoter never hints that he's already advertised. Now the promoter puts up a quick sign at the ticket window saying that you've canceled. Maybe next week's print ad will have a slash across the ad saying only, "Canceled." Now everybody figures that you're having problems, are unreliable, or couldn't sell enough to even go out. The negative reasons are so easily believed, but the actual reason never comes out.

I remember a saying, but not who said it. It paraphrases something like this: "The longer I'm in the art of music, the more I can appreciate the efforts of other musicians." In other words, the more I know, the more I can see of value in others' playing. Absolutely true. I've noticed a tremendous change over the years. I was a confused teenager when I wrote some of the stuff that ended up on our Dregs albums. I guarantee that not only have I widened my musical scope, but now I can see more good things around me. And now, I am way less tolerant of hearing that people hate others or their playing.

Next time you hear a bunch of musicians talkin' trash, throw in a positive comment just to spoil the party. One little push like that can change the direction of a conversation from gossip to constructive observation. If you still feel outnumbered, remember this: One of my good role model friends from the South said, "Yeah, we've all done it, but that don't make it right!" Think forward.

Contact
A Nutritious Breakfast Food

One thing about having contact with a lot of people that helps with this column is that many subjects are brought up, asked about, discussed. At a normal gig, a musician will most likely spend more time talking to people and answering questions than he will at playing. Exceptions would be if you show up just in time to do seven sets with 10 minute breaks, then split for home. Ditto for a concert where the musician needs near-total isolation, plays, and then takes off. Most musicians, though, end up with quite a bit of contact with their audience, partly because of the access of a club atmosphere.

That contact, that feedback from an audience, is extremely valuable. It's how we learn what really goes over well and what doesn't when we're up on stage. After all, in a club you're close enough to evaluate a good percentage of the audience with your own eyes and ears. You'll definitely be able to see the reactions written on people's faces, too. That can be more important than just judging the reaction on the applause decibels. Very important, too, will be the comments from some of the quietest members of the audience. These are often intense people, maybe musicians, who will give you some challenging questions and some serious critique. I've always found that it's fun to hear what people think after a gig, partly because people who go to shows have a real love for the excitement of live music. When there are a lot of people to talk to, naturally the time of contact with each person can get very short out of necessity. On rare occasions, someone will think that there is an unlimited time frame to hang out and talk, because they aren't aware of all the other things that need to happen. They might take offense that they can't spend more time, and might judge you harshly as a result, but all people can't share exactly the same sense of fair play.

Over the years, I've gotten suggestions for columns, encouragement to tackle the impossible (e.g., stay the musical course with the Dregs), a sense of what music means to those who enjoy it, and some genuine inspiration. From the people. I often get asked what I listen to, and I have to say that I listen to people with as much interest as to most music. I have accumulated a gigantic backlog of demos passed on to me, mostly because it would take another hour or two a day just to keep up, let alone catch up.

Usually, though, I have a chance to talk to those people who hand me their tapes or CD's, and I always encourage them to keep making recordings from which to learn and chart their progress. I've never been a letter writer, and I really don't write letters to my parents or brothers, and I love them dearly. I usually tell that to those who want a written critique sent back to them, hoping that they'll understand. At some point in my life, it would be good for me to become a critic and coach, maybe. But not while the minutes are racing by, competing for time with my son, practice time, sleep, essential chores, and an absolute barrage of phone calls, despite delegating some things to my friends who help me take care of portions of my business decisions.

Still, those people are what make those few hours a week into performances. Without those people, it would be just a dress rehearsal; there's no need to travel all over the world to do that. That's why most concerts involve not just the practice time at the hotel, the phone interviews, travel, workshops (clinics), and signing and picture taking in the lobby. Besides all that stuff, the time at the gig itself can easily be five to six hours for a two-hour show. That's because there are plenty of people behind the scenes with requests, too. Relations with the promoter, sponsors, contest winners, record company reps, and guests are important parts of a professional musician's responsibilities. But it's the people who have chosen to dig in their pockets, wait in line for tickets, trudge from distant parking, endure sometimes harsh outdoor conditions, and still give energy to give the show, who you want to thank, too.

Working with Deep Purple, an extremely international group, for the past half decade, I've been to a number of gigs where we were cut off from any contact with the audience. This is usually because the dressing rooms at some outdoor concerts are driving distance away, or crowd control is done by the military or police, or sometimes because there's no place to meet and greet. Sometimes, the schedule forces a drive back to the hotel immediately after walking off stage. Invariably, it feels strange to have that part of the process, the contact, taken away. The near-instantaneous arrival back at the hotel while still sweaty from the show seems out of synch with all those years of talking about the show in the dressing room with the band, then getting changed and meeting the hardcore fans to hear their likes, dislikes, and suggestions about the set.

Despite occasionally being beaten over the head with the fact that you can't please all the people you meet, I still say that it's not a real gig without that contact. If you don't think it's important, try doing what I do each morning: While looking at whatever breakfast food I'm eating, I can't help but wonder which audience member's wages paid for that food.

Getting the Message

There's this cartoon showing a dog's owner giving some commands to the dog. The guy is saying something like, "Rover, now you be a good boy and go get the newspaper for me. Okay, Rover?" Then it has a frame that shows what the dog actually processes from those words. It shows the dog looking at the guy and the word balloon coming from the guy's mouth says, "Rover, blah blah blah blah blah, blah, blah, blah, blah, Rover." It's been years since I've actually seen that cartoon, but that's kind of the essence, anyway. My point is that the dog didn't get the message, of course. What he did get was his name being said, nothing else.

I wonder how close people actually come to being like the dog when they listen to other musicians. It takes some effort sometimes to get the message instead of just hearing the riffs. Look at some examples. The classic ZZ Top tune, "La Grange," has a solo that sits on one note somewhere in the middle. While Billy Gibbons plays that note, he plays harmonics by changing the position of his right hand and pick. When people copy that solo, you will often hear them just play the same note repeatedly, and it doesn't feel right. To me, the actual thing that I get from that little section is that the same pitched note can be repeated, but still be interesting, if you change other things such as the harmonic tone, the intensity of the picking, or even the rhythm of the picking. In other words, one technique to use in soloing is to repeat one thing while you alter another facet of it. By the way, the fact that we guitarists can get so much variety from any one note could be the only thing keeping us from being sampled and replaced by synths.

If you got the same message from hearing that solo, you might try something besides just playing the same note over and over when you were imitating Billy's style. Better yet, you might try your own version of the same idea, such as playing the same pitch note but changing the string that you play it on every time you hit it; or changing octaves, or pickups, each time you strike the note. What about repeating a whole riff, but changing the octave each time, or changing from muted to un-muted picking each time? At that point, you're getting the message, not just parroting back what you heard.

Another example might be Stevie Ray Vaughn's style of playing. If you want to pick up some of what he had to say, don't just buy a hat, a Strat, and tune down a half step. Instead of imitating the external things, try to get the message. The way I might look at it is that it sounds great to play on the relaxed part of the beat with very rhythmic, insistent phrasing. Even from the obvious physical equipment that he played, regardless of which brand of guitar you play, there's something to be said for playing a heavier gauge string: It gives an immediate quality to each note. Sure, the notes are easier to bend with the thinner strings, but the heavier ones reward you with a fatter sound and more punch.

I'm heavily influenced by the Beatles, but nothing I write sounds particularly like them. That's because rather than using the same progressions or riffs, I get a more general sense of what I like about them. Their harmonies, for instance, always changed between being parallel thirds, to fifths, or sixths, all in the same phrase. The point here is that having some unpredictable character adds interest to any part of music, when used in the right amounts. If you listen to Bach, you might get the same message without necessarily copping his phrases.

Now, let's turn the tables and use an example that may have happened to you. Your friend has just made a suggestion that you add a bridge section to the tune you're trying to write together. So far, the tune is in A, and he wants to play the new section in B♭. You try it, and it doesn't sound good to you, so you inform him that his idea sucks. Wait a minute: Give his actual suggestion a good try. What he really could be suggesting is that the tune needs a key change at that point. If B♭ doesn't do it, try all the other keys and see if you can find one that sounds perfect. That way, instead of putting him down and making him feel worthless, you have gotten some inspiration from him to find something new. In other words, you find that the message, not the exact example of it, may work. That is, the key change could really be cool, but the key of B♭ was only the first one to try.

Another bit of advice that I know you can use is about working on lyrics. If somebody suggests a couple of phrases that sound like they should be in a nursery rhyme, don't throw the idea out. Maybe the message is that the rhythmic construction of the line, or the number of syllables, made the person feel strongly enough to suggest them in the first place. Try exchanging the words for similar-feeling words that you can live with. If people are really brainstorming with each other, they don't guard everything they say; they speak as soon as they have an idea. One way to kill the brainstorming session is to put down someone else's idea and dismiss it with a, "Nah, that's no good." Try this: "I like the idea of what you're suggesting. Can we change the words, but stick with that idea?"

Maybe one in a thousand people can naturally do this kind of thing; the rest of us learn it. The sooner the better.

Guitar one™

The Magazine You Can Play

CHERRY LANE
MUSIC COMPANY

Visit the Guitar One web site at www.guitarone.com

GuitarOne Presents • The Best Bass Lines INCLUDES TAB

Get the low-down on the low-end sounds from 24 super songs, straight from the pages of *GuitarOne* magazine! Includes note-for-note bass transcriptions with tab for: Badge • Bohemian Rhapsody • Celebrity Skin • Crash into Me • Crazy Train • Everything Zen • Glycerine • Jerry Was a Race Car Driver • Money • November Rain • Smoke on the Water • Suffragette City • Sweet Child O' Mine • Violet • What Would You Say • You're My Flavor • and more.

_____02500311 Play-It-Like-It-Is Bass $14.95

GuitarOne Presents • Blues Licks for Guitar
by Chris Amelar

A great guide to blues improvisation that will fit in your guitar case! This book will help you develop a strong blues vocabulary by teaching many of the licks and phrases essential to playing blues solos. Also examines scales used in blues improv, and techniques like bending and vibrato. Includes an intro by guitar pro Chris Amelar, and a complete 12-bar blues solo at the end of the book. 4½" x 12"

_____02500118..$5.95

GuitarOne Presents • Blues Rockers INCLUDES TAB

12 rockin' blues favorites, including: Changes • I Can't Quit You Baby • Jingo (Jin-Go-Lo-Ba) • Ramblin' Man • Smoking Gun • Steppin' Out • Tightrope • and more.

_____02500264 Play-It-Like-It-Is Guitar $14.95

GuitarOne Presents • Legends of Lead Guitar
The Best of Interviews: 1995-2000

Who can explain the extensive thought processes and flights of fancy by which a virtuoso guitarist makes a metal, wood & wire contraption sing, snarl, whisper or weep? None but the artist. Hence this book. *Legends of Lead Guitar* is a fascinating compilation of *GuitarOne* magazine interviews with today's greatest lead guitarists – and your backstage pass to the art of the rock'n'roll axe! From deeply rooted blues giants to the most fearless pioneer, legendary players reveal how they achieve their extraordinary craft. Artists featured include: AC/DC • Aerosmith • Jeff Beck • Black Crowes • Bush • Coal Chamber • Collective Soul • Creed • Deftones • Ani DiFranco • Kevin Eubanks • Foo Fighters • Goo Goo Dolls • Buddy Guy • Eric Johnson • Kid Rock • B.B. King • Kiss • Korn • Lenny Kravitz • Limp Bizkit • Metallica • Dave Navarro • Jimmy Page • Pantera • Les Paul • Rage Against the Machine • Red Hot Chili Peppers • Carlos Santana • Kenny Wayne Shepherd • Andy Summers • Third Eye Blind • Steve Vai • Eddie Van Halen • and more!

_____02500329 ....$19.95

GuitarOne Presents • Lesson Lab

This exceptional book/CD pack features more than 20 in-depth lessons from the pages of *GuitarOne* magazine's most popular department. Tackle a variety of pertinent music- and guitar-related subjects, such as scales, chords, theory, guitar technique, songwriting, and much more!

_____02500330 Book/CD Pack.............................$19.95

Prices, contents, and availability subject to change without notice.

GuitarOne Presents • Noise and Feedback

_____02500328 ....$16.95

GuitarOne Presents • Rock Legends INCLUDES TAB

Transcriptions with tab for 21 rock classics from some of the greatest guitarists ever! Includes: All Along the Watchtower (Hendrix) • Badge (Cream) • Crazy on You (Heart) • Crazy Train (Osbourne) • Flying in a Blue Dream (Satriani) • Hide Away (Clapton) • Hot Blooded (Foreigner) • Sweet Child O' Mine (Guns N' Roses) • Telephone Song (Stevie Ray Vaughan) • You Really Got Me (Van Halen) • and more.

_____02500262 Play-It-Like-It-Is Guitar $14.95

GuitarOne Presents • Signature Songs INCLUDES TAB

This cool collection features 21 artists and note-for-note transcriptions of the hit songs that remind us of them! Includes: Aerosmith, "Walk This Way" • Cream, "Sunshine of Your Love" • Guns N' Roses, "Welcome to the Jungle" • Dave Matthews Band, "What Would You Say" • Ozzy Osbourne, "Crazy Train" • Santana, "Smooth" • Van Halen, "You Really Got Me" • The Who, "My Generation" • and more!

_____02500303 Play-It-Like-It-Is Guitar $16.95

GuitarOne Presents • Studio City • *by Carl Verheyen*

Professional guitarist Carl Verheyen chronicles his career as one of L.A.'s top-call session players in this complete collection of his Studio City columns from *Guitar* magazine. He draws on his vast experience to advise guitarists how to: exercise studio etiquette and act professionally • acquire, assemble and set up gear for sessions • use the tricks of the trade to become a studio hero • get repeat call-backs • and much more. This is the handbook for recording guitarists who want a career as a professional studio player!

_____02500195 ....$9.95

Visit Cherry Lane Online at **www.cherrylane.com**